The Moravian Springplace Mission to the Cherokees, Abridged Edition

The Word
was mad
Flesh

Indians of the Southeast

The Moravian Springplace Mission to the Cherokees,

ABRIDGED EDITION

Edited and with an introduction by

Rowena McClinton

UNIVERSITY OF NEBRASKA PRESS
LINCOLN AND LONDON

Manufactured in the
United States of America
♾

Frontispiece. Early nineteenth-century watercolor by Anna Rosina (née Kliest) Gambold depicting a Christmas celebration at the Bethlehem Female Seminary for Young Ladies. Courtesy of the Moravian Archives, Bethlehem, Pennsylvania.

Library of Congress
Cataloging-in-Publication Data
Gambold, Anna Rosina, d. 1821.
The Moravian Springplace Mission to the Cherokees / edited and with an introduction by Rowena McClinton.—Abridged ed.
p. cm.—(Indians of the Southeast)
Includes bibliographical references.
ISBN 978-0-8032-2095-9 (paper: alk. paper)
1. Cherokee Indians—Missions—Georgia—Spring Place—History—19th century—Sources. 2. Moravians—Missions—Georgia—Spring Place—History—19th century—Sources. 3. Cherokee Indians—Georgia—Spring Place—History—19th century—Sources. 4. Indian school children—Georgia—Spring Place—History—19th century—Sources. 5. Gambold, John, ca. 1761–1827—Diaries. 6. Gambold, Anna Rosina, d. 1821—Diaries. 7. Moravians—Georgia—Spring Place—Diaries. 8. Missionaries—Georgia—Spring Place—Diaries. 9. Springplace Mission (Ga.)—History—19th century—Sources. 10. Spring Place (Ga.)—History—19th century—Sources.
I. McClinton, Rowena, 1940– II. Gambold, John, ca. 1761–1827. III. Title.
E99.C5G164 2010
266'.467583108997557—dc22
2010017331

Set in Adobe Garamond

To the memory of my grandfather Samuel Proctor McRae

Contents

Maps

Series Editors' Preface

The Moravians, a pietistic German sect who settled in piedmont North Carolina in the mid-eighteenth century, conducted the first sustained Christian missionary work among the Cherokees. The mission's most dynamic years were those when John and Anna Rosina Gambold provided its leadership. The Gambold years correspond to a period of enormous change in Cherokee society. In this period, the Cherokees became increasingly engaged in a commercial agricultural economy, coped with land cession and removal, and began to centralize their government. At the same time, many traditional beliefs and practices endured. The missionaries were witnesses to this tumultuous time, and they recorded their impressions in the mission diary. Like the missionaries of other denominations, they were sometimes ethnocentric and condescending, and they often wrote about activities, such as medical treatments and ball games, of which they did not approve. By recording the Cherokee life they observed every day, however, they have left us a valuable record of cultural persistence and social transformation. They also have given us a portrait of themselves, and the kindness and generosity that is evident in this diary explains why many Cherokees addressed the Gambolds as "mother" and "father."

The abridged edition of the Moravian Springplace Mission to the

Cherokees provides an annotated translation of the mission diary during the period of the Gambolds' tenure. Because the Moravians wrote their journals in German, their native language, these documents have not been readily accessible to many people interested in their content. Recognizing their value, the Moravian Archives in Winston-Salem, North Carolina, generously permitted Rowena McClinton to prepare this scholarly edition. McClinton used both her own translations and those done in house, and she brought to the project not only her facility with German script but also her deep understanding of Cherokee and Moravian history. Her training enabled her to decipher oblique references to the Cherokees' matrilineal kinship system, medico-religious practices, and other cultural expressions as well as Moravian notions about salvation, the lot, Christ's wounds, community, and propriety. This volume conveys her respect for both cultures as well as for the complex cultural interactions of the people who appear on these pages. Her annotations make this diary particularly useful to scholars, but they also will make the diary accessible to a wide range of readers. We are pleased to welcome this work to the Indians of the Southeast Series.

—*Theda Perdue*
Michael D. Green
University of North Carolina, Chapel Hill

Acknowledgments

Many persons made suggestions and assisted me in the publication of *The Moravian Springplace Mission to the Cherokees, Abridged Edition.* Past acquisitions editor and director of the University of Nebraska Press Gary Dunham, now of Albany, New York, recommended that I write a thematic abridgment of the *Moravian Springplace Mission to the Cherokees* (2 vols., Nebraska, 2007), similar to *An American Epic of Discovery: The Lewis and Clark Journals: The Abridgment of the Definitive Nebraska Edition* (Nebraska, 2003) edited and with introduction by Gary E. Moulton. Present editor-in-chief and acquisitions editor Heather Lundine has assisted me in expediting the publication process. The expert attention copyeditor Lona Dearmont had applied to the reading and correcting of the two-volume *Moravian Springplace Mission to the Cherokees* allowed me to extract themes with less difficulty than otherwise.

I am most appreciative of everyone who works at the Newberry Library. I use the extensive collections regularly, and the use of a Newberry carrel has allowed me to conduct the needed research for this project. Newberry Library's John Aubry shared his finely tuned knowledge of the Ayer Collection and Native Americans in general, which enhanced my ability to comprehend the complexities and nuances of the two volumes. Overall, the Newberry's Research and Education staff, in particular director Jim

Grossman, assistant director Diane Dillon, and Leslie Kan, make available an ongoing scholarly community. The Newberry's Center for Renaissance Studies gave me a generous grant for the project "Moravian Roots and Culture" that augmented the religious sections of the *Moravian Springplace Diary, Abridged Edition*. I am grateful to the center's director, Carla Zecher, and assistant director Karen Christianson. The Newberry Library has also bestowed on me the honor of scholar in residence.

Productive travels to the Moravian Archives in Winston-Salem, North Carolina, and Bethlehem, Pennsylvania, have led to more substantive information about the life of Anna Rosina Gambold. I am grateful to archivist Dr. C. Daniel Crews and assistant archivist Richard Starbuck of Winston-Salem, archivists Paul Peucker and Laney Graf of Bethlehem, and former archivist Vernon Nelson.

The publication of the original volumes of the *Moravian Springplace Mission to the Cherokees* has led to speaking engagements, and on these occasions, I have had the opportunity to share the publication's depiction of early nineteenth-century Cherokees and their cultural traditions. The following leaders and organizations have imparted valuable comments that have prompted a deeper understanding of Cherokees' significant place in history: David Hampton, president of the Descendants of Nancy Ward Association; Jack Baker, president of the National Trail of Tears Association; Sandy Boaz, president of the Illinois chapter of the Trail of Tears; William Furry, executive director of the Illinois State Historical Society; Mike Batanski, executive board member of the Illinois State Historical Society; Anna Smith, president of the Cherokee Moravian Historical Society; and Tim Howard, president of the Murray County Historical Society.

Conversations with colleagues Tiya A. Miles, Patsy Edgar, Ada Deer, Marybelle Chase, Sarah Hill, Tim Garrison, Julie Autry, Jeff Stencil, Duane King, Theda Perdue, Mike Green, Jamie Paxton, Thomas McCraw, Fred Hoxie, LaVonne Ruoff, Loretta Fowler, Raymond Fogelson, Helen Tanner, David Nichols, Gwynne Henderson, Cheryl Jett, Lorri Glover, Dan Smith, and Ella Drake have opened new approaches to the study of Native peoples in contact with Anglo America. My place of work, Southern Illinois University Edwardsville, has encouraged a caring, collegial workplace. I am especially grateful to Carl Springer, associate dean of the College of Arts and Sciences; to Sheryl Lauth and Edwin Franklin of the Faculty Technology Center; to fellow members of the Department of Historical Studies; and to department chair and associate professor Anthony Cheeseboro.

My family has given me confidence to stay the course. I am very grateful to my three daughters, Rowena, Holly, and Kathryn, my father, Raymond McClinton, my brother, Raymond McClinton, my uncle, Richard McRae, and my cousin Vaughan McRae, all of whom have been generous in their encouragement. I also want to thank numerous friends who are unnamed but are still an indelible and constant source of spirit and strength.

Editorial Policy

This abridgment of *The Moravian Springplace Mission to the Cherokees, 1805–1821*, is a representative compilation of Anna Rosina Gambold's written observations extracted from the recently published two-volume edition. Anna Rosina Gambold was the principal writer from October 1, 1805, to June 30, 1820, but other missionaries wrote from time to time: Gottlieb Byhan kept the diary from January 1, 1805, to October 1, 1805, and Anna Rosina's husband, John, wrote during the periods April 1 to September 30, 1812; August 1 to November 2, 1813; and July 22 to October 31, 1816. After Anna Rosina's illness and subsequent death on February 21, 1821, John left Springplace Mission in March of 1821, when he was reassigned to Oothcaloga, a newly opened Moravian Cherokee mission some thirty miles south of Springplace. To complete the entire tenure of the Gambold years, the year 1821 is included in this edition. Beginning in the summer of 1820, Johannes Renatus Schmidt and his wife, Gertraud Salome, came to Springplace from New Fairfield, Canada; however, Salem archivist Rev. Dr. Crews, assistant archivist Mr. Starbuck, and I cannot with certainty discern the handwriting from July 1, 1820, through the year 1821. Various missionaries' handwritings checked against letters they wrote to members of the Salem congregation made positive identity a certainty except in the aforementioned instance.[1]

Transcribed and translated from approximately 1,490 pages of German script, an archaic writing convention, the English translations in the two-volume edition adhered to precision rather literary grace.[2] Springplace Diary narratives remained unaltered, and brackets were used for dates and sometimes clarification. Editorially, I used ellipses to signal the omission of words and sentences superfluous to content narrative and overall meaning of the passages. I chose to delete endemic references to the Savior and included them only if germane to the overall message of the particular passage. The centerpiece for this project is the ethnographic literature found within the Springplace Diary. For this abridgment, mainly Cherokee persons and voices are chronicled even though there is a wealth of information about Cherokee slaves and Cherokee slaveholding.[3]

Choosing an organizational pattern for this abridgment was problematic mainly because Anna Rosina considered the Cherokee worldview as tangential to her role as evangelical missionary. But regardless of her focus, ethnographic materials are prevalent throughout, and choosing what topics to include and then sorting through substantive materials to determine their gravity made the project even more challenging. After many perusals of the two-volume edition of the Springplace Diary, two concepts emerged that could encompass two complementary but separate paths. Ever mindful that the Cherokee voice would surface and be heard, I chose the chapter titles "Significant Events and Themes at Springplace Mission between 1805 and 1821" and "Continuity of Traditional Cherokee Cultural Traits."

Primarily, the significant events and cultural encounters addressed in the first chapter resulted from missionary presence and the United States' Indian policies. These events and encounters occurred both because of and regardless of the mission's existence; many of those giving rise to narratives occurred within the mission's environs. As an educational, religious, and political presence, alien and anomalous to the Cherokees, Springplace Mission and its missionaries served as a magnet for conversions, rejections of Christianity, annuity distributions at neighbor James Vann's plantation and elsewhere, happenings within the mission itself resulting from students' sicknesses, truancy, parents removing their offspring, rumors of missionary ill-treatment, students' "errant" behavior, a student's death, and notable visitors. Other western-oriented influences discussed widely were uses of alcohol. The second part of the first chapter concentrates on happenings of national importance and influence: the 1811–12 New Madrid earthquake and aftershocks and the 1813–14 Creek War. In other words, in the first chapter, careful attention was given to comings and goings that were happenstance to Cherokees as a whole and not necessarily Cherokee in origin.

In contrast, the second chapter addresses intrinsic Cherokee traditions, values, and undertakings that survived missionary and U.S. government influence and presence. Spiritual discourses Cherokees held with Anna Rosina revealed that the Cherokees did have a rootedness in their own spirituality. This chapter reinforces the Cherokee concept of land, Cherokee agricultural practices, matrilineality, body ornaments, marriages, healing and conjuring, rainmaking, death and burial customs, trade, Cherokee law and punishments, responses to Christian images, Green Corn ceremony, ball play, and Cherokee origin stories.

In both chapters themes do overlap. For example, alcohol use was present at ball play and at annuity distributions; Cherokee origin stories integrated Cherokee attachment to land and its resources; healing prompted issues of matrilineality; the hiring of conjurors included Cherokee use of corporal punishment. Almost every topic has a subsection with a Cherokee (sometimes an American) person named (when known) as a source for or author of that narrative. When further content explanation seemed appropriate, I have included a short narrative.

An epilogue redirects the reader to Cherokee identity and survival in the American South. Moravian missionaries John Gambold and Johannes Renatus Schmidt wrote poignant reflections considering whether forced removal was just ahead.

The Moravian Springplace Mission to the Cherokees, Abridged Edition

Introduction

This abridgment of the two-volume *Moravian Springplace Mission to the Cherokees* illuminates the careful observations of Anna Rosina née Kliest Gambold, Moravian missionary to the Cherokees from 1805 to 1821. Recorded almost daily, the narratives are extracted from the two volumes of *The Moravian Springplace Mission to the Cherokees, 1805–1813 and 1814–1821*. The entries reflect the interactions, at Springplace Mission, of mainly two disparate groups, the Unity of the Brethren or *Brüdergemeine* (later named Moravian),[1] and the Cherokees. A bilingual, dissident religious community stemming from German heritage, the *Brüdergemeine* promoted a religion of heartfelt feeling, a contrite heart, humility, and unconditional devotion to the crucified Christ. The other group, the early nineteenth-century Cherokees living in parts of the present-day states of Tennessee, North Carolina, Georgia, and Alabama, had emerged from centuries' old Mississippian traditions that imbued the physical world with spiritual meaning and preserved a highly refined system of balance and order. Their very rocks and streams held life that transcended the secular Anglo-American world that would displace them in the infamous Trail of Tears, the 1838–39 forced removal. Against this backdrop of heightened tensions over United States' dispossession of Cherokees from ancestral domains, one particular Moravian missionary, Anna Rosina, took her pedagogical talents, intellect, people skills, and devotion to Christianity to the Cherokee Nation and lived among the Cherokees at Springplace, a present-day site in northwestern Georgia.[2]

Nestled in the valley between ridges and low, rounded, pockmarked mountains that formed the Appalachians, dating back some 750 million years, Springplace was so named for its abundance of waters, seven bubbling limestone springs, three of which were on the thirty-five-acre property. The region's springs flowed out of limestone beds into a creek that led to the Conasauga River, a tributary of the Coosa.[3]

Though seemingly isolated in the lower reaches of the Appalachian Mountains, this particular Cherokee land faced unabated encroachment. Providing inducements to settlers were the extraordinary fertility of the soil and a healthy climate, the finest climate reported to be on the border between Tennessee and Georgia.[4] Knowing the dire circumstances Indians faced from settler incursion on Indian lands and resources, policy makers George Washington and Henry Knox were the initial ones to foster a series of Trade and Intercourse Acts (1790–1823) to assist the Indians in assimilating with Anglo-Americans. Providing "arts of civilization" also included offering incentives to Moravian missionaries to dwell among Indians.[5] Expediency was key to Cherokee elders because they knew that their children faced a world far more complicated and complex—a world filled with land-hungry settlers poised to dislodge the Indians from their hereditary domains. So to forestall removal and support the Cherokees' maintaining their ties to the Southeast, the Moravians acquiesced to Cherokee demands to teach Cherokee young people English, not German. The Cherokees told the Moravians they had no ear for religion, but their admonitions failed to discourage evangelization. By 1801 the Moravians completed Springplace Mission, conveniently located near the road leading to Tellico (near present-day Knoxville, Tennessee) and just sixteen miles north of Oostanaula (later the capital named New Echota), one of several sites where the Cherokees' National Council met.[6]

Springplace, centrally located in the Cherokee Nation, served as a welcoming center on the Federal Road[7] connecting Augusta, Georgia, to Nashville, Tennessee.[8] In 1800, when Moravian missionaries accepted the invitation from the Cherokees, representatives of Upper Town Cherokee chief James Vann[9] and Lower Town chiefs Doublehead[10] and Little Turkey[11] agreed to loan the Moravians land and let Vann sell them the improvements. The lot[12] ultimately decided on the Vann site among the Upper Town Cherokees for the mission.[13]

On their way to Springplace, husband and wife team John and Anna Rosina Gambold were welcomed by Lower Town leader Doublehead at Southwest Point,[14] the headquarters of the Indian agent to the Cherokees, Colonel Return Jonathan Meigs.[15] Doublehead told the Gambolds that he hoped our "intercourse with our nearest neighbors, who are wild, might have a good influence on them."[16] Arriving by wagon and horseback on October 26, 1805, the Gambolds, principal missionaries for seventeen years, brought the "arts of civilization"—reading, writing, arithmetic, and Christianity—to the Cherokees. These were the very activities that governmental agents deemed worthy for "civilized" life. To U.S. policy makers, the Cherokees appeared primed as a people prepared to accept European instruction. Anna Rosina assisted Cherokee youth to learn skills amenable to U.S. policy makers as ways to value Cherokees as "civilized" and therefore worthy to remain in their homeland; she taught the sons and daughters of leading Cherokee families, The Hair, Rattling Gourd, James Vann, The Ridge, David Watie, and Charles and William Hicks.[17]

The spectacular life of Anna Rosina Gambold reflected the many trials and contributions of the *Brüdergemeine* in mid-eighteenth-century British North America. Born in Bethlehem on May 1, 1761,[18] she witnessed in her younger years vast changes in the *Brüdergemeine* as the members wrestled intensely from the effects wrought by the "sifting period," their undue obsession with wound theology, and the demise of a communal economy.[19] Though the founder of the Renewed Moravian Church, Saxon count Nicholas Ludwig von Zinzendorf, had died the year before Anna Rosina's birth, Bethlehem and the worldwide Unity of the Brethren had not completely forsaken the practice of communalism, as the choir system was still in place.[20] Anna Rosina's parents, as a married couple, experienced the highly regulated choir or band system, a communal economy that was idiosyncratic to the Moravians, instituted by Count von Zinzendorf. Zinzendorf's Bethlehem, founded in 1741, divided its congregation into ten choirs: single men, single women,[21] older boys, older girls, little boys, little girls, married men, married women, widowers, and widows. He believed that the choir institution corresponded to the stages of the Savior's life from infancy to manhood. Christ became the model for the phases of human life (marriage was for procreation purposes only) as Moravians applied His meritorious sacrifices to their earthly existence.[22] Furthermore, the choir system had utilitarian purposes. It expedited travel, lessened Zinzendorf's financial outlay, and called for less land on which to live. In the case of Anna Rosina's parents, married couples lived in their respective choirs but were allowed to come together at appointed times by means of a small room and corridor connecting the Married Men's Choir with the Married Women's in these dwellings.[23]

Choirs also served educational needs because they trained and educated the youth. Moravian offspring became property of the church, and the congregation expected them to assist the spiritual institution that had nurtured them in childhood and adolescence. These pervasive practices grew out of the belief that the Moravian Church had first claim on members' destinies. Eventually communicants focused on missionary activity, and they poured their energy into evangelicalism whether they actually participated or not. These determinants diluted the family circle, but training and sending members to foreign mission fields met little or no resistance.[24]

When Anna Rosina came of age, she entered the Single Sisters'[25] Choir and lived there until the lot chose John Gambold to be her husband.[26] The choir system was all-consuming; the Single Sisters represented a large family whose choir duties included sewing, washing, ironing, and the growing of apples, strawberries, white raspberries, gooseberries, and currants.[27] Sister Anna Rosina labored with the other Sisters in "an exclusive organization in which prevailed a communism not of goods but of labor."[28] Throughout the Bethlehem community, women served as nurses, teachers, seamstresses, laundresses, cooks, maids, gardeners, and caretakers of livestock. Women nurtured each other, both physically and spiritually, from birth to death. Women were taught by women; young girls were tutored by women. In ceremonies, females administered such rituals as communion and foot washing to fellow females. Women held their "speakings"[29] with one another whereby they unbosomed their hearts to the female superintendent, or *Vorsteherin*, of the Single Sisters' house.[30]

Moravian historian and scholar Katherine M. Faull elucidates that female self-awareness and self-consciousness arose not from autonomous reasoning but from each woman's communication with the congregation and from her communion with the Savior. Additionally, Zinzendorf contended that women were more receptive than men of the "right" feelings for what he thought constituted religion. He believed that when Jesus appeared again, He would appear to a woman first because she possessed the qualities that would enable her to appreciate what it meant to be *Keuschheit*, or chaste. To sustain their chastity, women were to carry a picture of Mary.[31] Even if married, a woman had to maintain her sense of virginity in order to be pure for Jesus.[32] In Moravian theology, the feminine realm was so revered that they believed that all souls were feminine and thus could be united with Christ as the husband after death.[33]

So in tune was she with her purposeful, driven inner life that when the *Brüdergemeine* faced external turbulence during the American Revolutionary War, she as an adolescent prepared herself for a teaching career in painting, poetry, and botany. Zinzendorf had encouraged opportunities for females to attain careers outside their quasi-monastic dwellings. In 1788 she joined the newly founded Moravian Female Seminary for Young Ladies at Bethlehem (1785). As a teacher, her first class was in one of the fine arts, where she was the first instructor of painting. Furthermore, her penchant for all the arts surfaced, particularly her poetic talent. As a poetess, she was in demand for the love-feasts and other celebrations.[34] Rhyming came easy to Anna Rosina, as some of her verse has been preserved. A pupil in the boarding school, Anna Allen, who was born December 6, 1780, and was the niece of Ethan Allen of Revolutionary War note (he visited Bethlehem May 13, 1778) and the daughter of Levi and Ann Allen, died on May 22, 1795. At her burial, Sister Anna Rosina Kliest wrote the following (extracted from the entire poem):

> 'Tis Anna's voice! Yes, blessed soul, we'll try
> Our lamps with oil here richly to supply.
> Faith in the Lamb for wretched sinners slain,
> Oh, may we, by his boundless grace, obtain![35]

At a public examination on May 13, 1789, the female pupils gathered to answer questions about English and German readings, grammar, and arithmetic. They distributed specimens of writing among the guests. A composition by Cornelia Lott Greene, daughter of Revolutionary War hero General Nathanael Greene, described Sister Kliest as having "rare skill clothing the ideas of her poetic fancy in the garb of a simple diction, such as falls naturally and forcibly on the ears of childhood."[36]

Her other skills included botany.[37] It was her great love for natural beauty as provided by the Bethlehem hillsides banking the Lehigh River that allowed her to express herself openly to her pupils outside of confining structures. She took her students on planned hillside walks and excursions along the Lehigh, including moonlight trips on the ferry. On these forays she spoke of the natural objects they saw around them: the many kinds of wildflowers, the ancient forest trees, the passing clouds, the twinkling stars, and even the stones—the science that lay behind all of these was politely shown, and tactfully under the guise of pleasure, her pupils learned the secrets of nature.[38]

Her experiences at Bethlehem prepared the way for her future commitment to Indian tribes; in 1803 she caught the attention of the recently (1802) arrived Moravian bishop, George Henry Loskiel of Herrnhut, Germany. No doubt he noted her success as a botany teacher and poetess, and her passion for the outdoors. Loskiel's knowledge of North American Indians was obtained by the copious church accounts Moravians generated about their worldwide missions in America and in far-flung regions such as Russia, Africa, and Greenland.[39] In his capacity as both bishop and newly elected president of the Helpers' Conference at Bethlehem, Loskiel decided in 1803 to take his wife, Maria Magdalena (née Barlach), and Sister Anna Rosina Kliest on a journey to Goshen, in Tuscarawas County, Ohio, to observe Indian missions firsthand and hold a mission conference[40] with Moravian missionary brethren David Zeisberger (the noted Apostle of the Indian, whom Anna Rosina called "patriarch of the fold"), John Heckewelder, John Benjamin Haven, John Schnall, and Benjamin Mortimer. The travelers expressed intense excitement encountering for the first time in the Ohio woods men and women about whom Loskiel had written while in Herrnhut.

The foray into interior America through Pennsylvania to Pittsburgh, then across the three rivers into Ohio and to the Ohio and Tusawarawas rivers, prepared Anna Rosina for the three-hundred-mile trip she would take in the fall of 1805 from Salem to Springplace, Georgia. On this Ohio expedition, Anna Rosina served as diarist and private secretary to Loskiel, carefully describing both terrain and people. She even noted the area of Lititz, Pennsylvania, and a place called Mountjoy. The Alleghenies seemed like giant hills, roads were miserable and poor, and nightfall brought in rats to forage for food. Hardships along the way failed to discourage the sojourners.[41]

Anticipating her first contacts with Indians, Anna Rosina discloses her innermost feelings: Her desire to meet the "Red People,"[42] once feared by her, became her all-consuming goal. At the Goshen Mission, Indians and Moravians greeted one another with kisses; Indians prepared fine lodging and food. She described her complete joy among those "*brown* ones, whom she loved," that such joy "could not be moved."[43] Anna Rosina met Delaware Indian convert William Henry, or Gelelemend, and other Indians from the "brown flock."[44] Indian and Moravian encounters in the Ohio and Pennsylvania valleys led to Indian esteem of the Moravians, setting them apart from other Americans and evangelical societies, thus permitting Moravian entry into Native communities.[45]

Zinzendorf's personal philosophy that promoting the worth of all humanity allowed him to conceptualize the "heathen"[46] in cultural, not racial, terms. His first contact with a "heathen" convert was in 1731 when he attended the coronation of Danish King Christian VI. He heard a baptized African slave,[47] Anthony Ulrich, relate that he had a sister in St. Thomas, "one of the Carybee islands belonging to the Danes, who wanted very much to learn Christianity."[48] Implementing his plans to organize missions among "neglected peoples," Zinzendorf sent the first set of Brethren missionaries, David Nitschmann and Leonard Dober, to St. Thomas in 1732 to preach among the African slaves.[49] As a closely knit congregation communicating continually about every event that communicants encountered, there is no doubt that Anna Rosina had heard the story of Anthony Ulrich many times. Zinzendorf's personal mission philosophy emanated from his belief in the innate worthiness[50] of all humans, and the application of this ideal came from earning esteem among the "heathen" with humility.[51]

Multiple mission enterprises reflected Moravian humble spirits and simplicity, transnational forces that went hand in hand with mission activity. Jon Sensbach, a scholar of Moravian missions among peoples of African descent, contends that eighteenth-century Moravian female converts of African heritage encountered equal opportunity and treatment as any of their white counterparts experienced. They went through open doors long after other religious groups had already shut them.[52] Before the hardening of racial lines and a growing sense of racialized gender roles in America during the nineteenth century, Moravians' acceptance of Indians, Creoles, and Africans into their membership was a widely held practice.[53] By the mid–eighteenth century, the Moravian Church ordained two women of African descent, Maria[54] and Rebecca.[55] By the early nineteenth century, another person by the name of Maria, Sister Maria Beaumont, a Moravian convert of African descent from the West Indies and a teacher, taught music at the Bethlehem Female Seminary. She received a Moravian education and lived in the Single Sisters' House.[56] Moravian females in the confines of the choir system became acquainted with the spiritual and eternal desires of their fellow beings from other cultures and concerned themselves with their attaining educational tools.[57] Though she lived in the Cherokee Nation at this time, Anna Rosina's exposure to her church's stand on intercultural tolerance allowed her to pursue a practical path in the Cherokee Nation that maximized her strengths as a teacher, lover of nature, and a tolerant participant in the dailiness of mission work.

Springplace missionaries brought to the Cherokee Nation the attribute of nonacquisitiveness that impressed the Reverend Elias Cornelius, a New England Congregational minister and United States negotiator to establish schools among the southeastern tribes. In the fall 1817, he wrote of his stay at Springplace: "I shall never forget this visit. These are good people. They have no interest of their own. . . . I seriously think that in the practice of godliness, in real humility, and self-denial they are the brightest ornaments of the Christian church."[58]

Also, Cornelius viewed the mission as belonging to the "civilized" world,"[59] with a school, a house for male students and visiting Cherokees, and two missionary dwellings. Other notable European influences looked upon as advancing "civilization" were the fence surrounding the property that held orderly and cleanly pruned apple and peach orchards, a vegetable garden to grow beans, squash, pumpkins, turnips, and sweet potatoes, a spacious springhouse to store milk, cheese, and butter, a flower garden, plant nursery, and two large fields for corn,[60] flax, oats, hay, and wheat. A labor-intensive small farm allowed the Moravians to become self-sufficient but simultaneously to garner the Cherokees' approbation, as each shared with the other varying foodstuffs and farm implements. The Moravians took their unused land and placed grazing animals—a few goats, sheep, pigs, and horned cattle—on it.[61] They had one or two horses to pull their wagon and haul firewood. The extensive use of animals and agricultural tools, and the vast variety of vegetable products just reinforced what Cornelius viewed as a highly cultivated place.[62]

Cornelius pinpointed the land directly in front of and surrounding John and Anna Rosina Gambold's house as "in the highest state of cultivation" and that Anna Rosina was "quite a botanist" with a "very good garden of plants, both ornamental and medicinal."[63] Anna Rosina's herb garden was widely used by Indians and non-Indians. Having learned the Linnaean classification system created by Swedish scientist Carl Linnaeus (1753), she had studied and taught plant life at the Female Seminary at Bethlehem, becoming one of the most well-known herbalists of her time.[64] What Cornelius noticed was a countryside improved by the hands of a female missionary whose agricultural endeavors had received considerable attention. Indeed, Cornelius described Springplace and its inhabitants as "a bright light in a dark, very dark place.[65]

Anna Rosina entered Cherokee country at an intense, ambiguous time when change was the only constant certainty. In the intimacy of the mission, she attested to what happened around her with a penchant for details that augmented her strength as a writer and passionate observer. Similar to John Heckewelder's ethnographies,[66] Anna Rosina's chronicled accounts of Indian manners and customs were from a missionary, like Heckewelder, "who was there."[67]

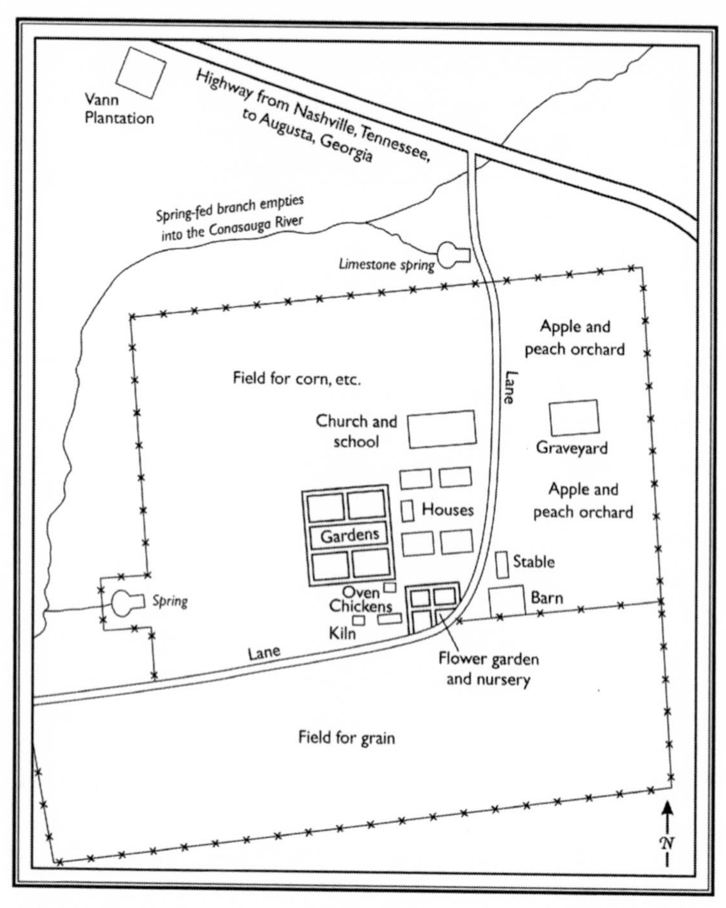

Map 1. Springplace Mission in 1819. Based on a drawing by Abraham Steiner published in Edmund Schwarze's *History of the Moravian Missions among Southern Indian Tribes of the United States*, courtesy of the Moravian Historical Society, Nazareth, Pennsylvania.

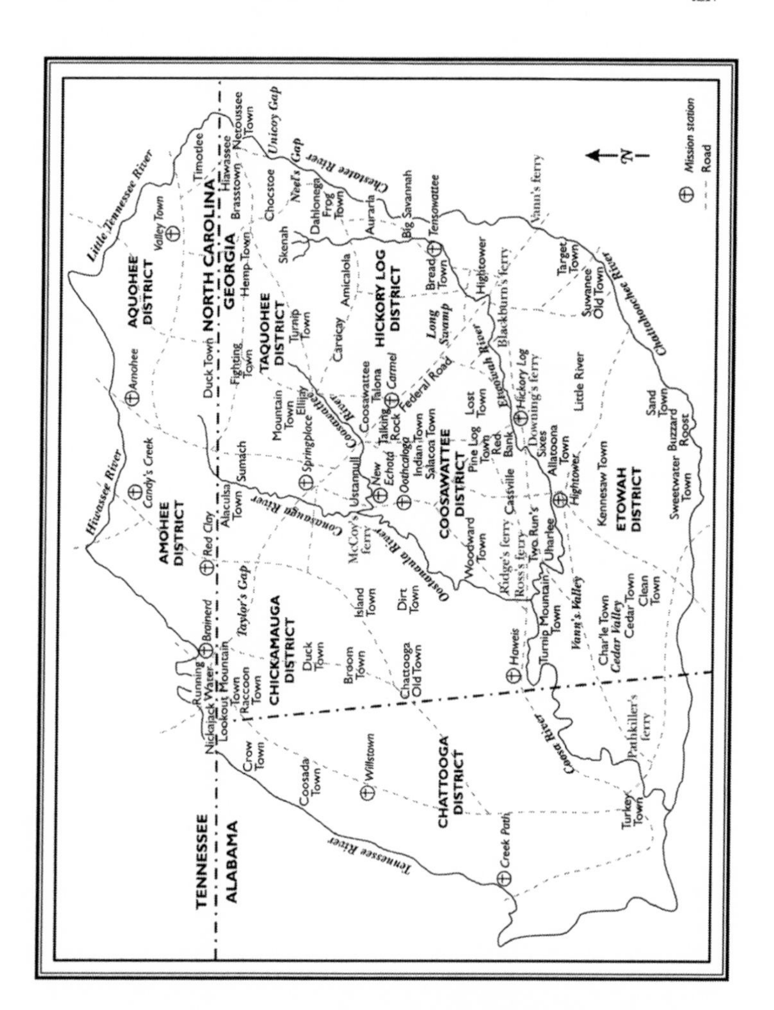

Map 2. Cherokee Nation, 1830. This map shows Cherokee boundaries, political districts, and the community locations that could be documented. Except for New Echota, most Cherokee communities consisted of farmsteads scattered along several miles of a river or creek. Based on a map drawn by Jeff Stancil of the Chief Vann House Historic Site; reproduced with permission.

1. Significant Events and Themes at Springplace Mission between 1805 and 1821

An imported enterprise, Springplace Mission not only mirrored western values but also showed how those very values intersected with and affected Cherokee sensibility. Though Anna Rosina's prime duty was to train Cherokee children in the "arts of civilization," the internal mission discourse ultimately reflected the intensity of disparate cultural contacts. The physicality of place allowed common ground where Cherokees and missionaries interacted and conversed. Those intense exchanges occurred in the mission school, in the barn that accommodated livestock and Christian services,[1] *in the Gambold residence that quartered female students, in separate housing for males, in the kitchen where the Moravians' slave, Pleasant, and her son, Michael, resided, or in the fields and gardens that provided produce for the missionaries, visitors, and Moravian students. Carefully observing what happened in the mission and beyond its environs, Anna Rosina chronicled the dailiness of mission life and what she heard and saw at Springplace.*

Conversion, Moravian Style

Zinzendorf's construction of mission morphology for indigenous peoples involved a tedious process, similar to the formulation of Puritan constructs as described by scholar of colonial Indian studies Daniel K. Richter.[2] *Initially, the Holy Spirit guided and directed the "heathen" to salvation. Then* without assistance from human agency, the Gambolds were mere agents of the Holy Spirit, while the Holy Spirit sought out "single souls" that Christ would choose for salvation. "Single souls" could be converted to the Moravian Church. Even if chosen for membership, "single souls" had to endure the tricky process of the lot. Then a convert still had other obstacles. In reality, the use of the lot promoted a "closed society" atmosphere, resembling a "club" with membership dependent upon social acceptance.[3]

The Gambolds employed severe means to determine the convert's sincerity before administering sacraments, especially Holy Communion.[4] One of these methods was das Sprechen ("speakings"), whereby "heathen" converts had to reveal the condition of their hearts. As spiritual leaders, the Gambolds encouraged "heathen" communicants to unveil contrite hearts, and unlike Catholic confession, divulge information beyond personal transgressions. Finally, at Springplace the Gambolds required that communicants notify them ahead of time if they could not attend services, and particularly, Holy Communion.[5]

Unlike eighteenth-century Moravian missionaries, the Gambolds were especially interested in converting prominent Cherokees because it would assure their staying power in the Cherokee Nation. The high profile of the Cherokees who did convert had a profound influence on the events in the Cherokee Nation and in the lives of the missionaries as well. On August 13,[6] 1810, the missionaries witnessed the "first fruit" of their labors, the conversion of Margaret Ann (Peggy) Vann Crutchfield (née Scott), the widow of Moravian patron and Cherokee leader James Vann. Charles Hicks, the uncle of Peggy Vann Crutchfield, attended her baptismal rites. Later he himself expressed an interest in becoming a Moravian. Hicks was baptized April 16, 1813, with the baptismal name Charles Renatus.[7]

A bilingual businessman, Hicks was also an interpreter for federal agents and missionaries, and he promoted education, commerce, and acculturation in general. In 1817 the National Council chose Hicks second principal chief and in 1827, principal chief. His presence at the Springplace services made missionaries intimately aware of Cherokee concerns and lent the mission effort credibility among the Cherokees. Many of the Cherokee students at Springplace had extensive kin connections throughout the nation including sometimes family ties with Hicks and his niece Peggy.[8]

Principal Converts to the Moravian Church

Margaret Ann Scott Vann Crutchfield

[August 1810] *On the 13th* on this important day of remembrance for the Unity of the Brethren[9] was the baptism of the first fruit[10] of the Cherokee Nation, our dear Peggy Scott, widow of James Vann. She invited her elder sister Betsy[11] and Uncle Charles Hicks as well as her mother[12] as witnesses for this grace intended for her. The latter, however, could not come, because she was not feeling well. When she arrived here in the morning dressed completely in white, we left her alone in a little room, as she wished, where we found her lying with her face down and her hands raised in a folded position.

She remained lying like this until she was brought in for the baptism. After her relatives and the Negro woman Candace, as well as all of our pupils, had gathered next to our small house in our barn, Brother Gambold began the service by singing the spiritual song, "Come Holy Ghost, come Lord our God!"[13] Meanwhile, the candidate was led in.

There soon arose a general crying, which occasionally interrupted the singing. This continued during Brother Gambold's address and prayer, especially when he thanked the dear Savior with childlike sincerity for this "first fruit." He commended her to His faithful hands for protection until the end and asked Him that more Cherokee souls would become the property of His salvation. Our dear Peggy answered the questions put to her before the baptism very sincerely with many tears. She was named Margaret Ann.[14] Her Negro Candace cried very loudly during the proceedings, as did her two younger sisters Isabel and Charlotte,[15] while their sister Peggy prayed. Oh, the feeling of the gracious presence of the Holy Trinity that prevailed during this first baptism in this country is indescribable.

It was really as if the place moved, yes, as if Jesus Christ, the crucified Son of God, stood there in the flesh and overflowed the souls thirsting for His blood. All those present were moved by grace. Shame and humiliation at such divine condescension filled each heart, and each one of us could do nothing more than cry and sigh. Here You have us all at your command, the more You command, the more victory we pay! Accept us as payment for Your pain and a thousand more hearts!

Mr. Charles Hicks,[16] who is our friend but did not attend any of our services on his last visit here, explained that he could not describe the feeling that he had experienced during this baptismal service. He said again upon leaving that he hoped that the impression of what he had enjoyed here today would stay with him the rest of his life.

Also he had another thorough discussion about baptism with Brother Gambold and asked a number of questions, which were answered to his satisfaction. He told us too that yesterday evening, some of the Vann relatives had come to Peggy's house to invite her to a ball play and other frolicking[17] today. They did not find her there since she was still at our place, so they had left a Negro behind with the message for her. She, however, turned this down with revulsion.

In the afternoon we had a visit from Mr. Brown,[18] Peggy's stepfather, and Mr. McNair.[19] When they learned what had taken place here today, both of them were very sorry that they had not come to us in the morning to attend the baptism.

In the evening, we once again thanked our dearest, gracious Savior on our knees for the grace we received today and asked Him for an increase of the payment for His pain through hearts from the poor Cherokee Nation as well. Afterward we had tasted an exceptionally blessed Holy Communion and our dear Margaret Ann came to us with her sister Betsy to see us and speak with us once again at the close of this, her great day of salvation.

Happy, like a quite blessed holy child, she talked with us a while about the great love and goodness of the dear Savior, especially to her, who herself had proved to be completely unworthy. We accompanied her on her way home all the way into the thicket and once again wished her a thousand blessings from the fullness of Jesus in her new life.

Our dear Brethren and Sisters[20] in all congregations will surely unite their thanks and praise with ours to our good Lord for this great mercy to this poor soul. At the same time, He will show to us, His unworthy children, who are convinced that they are not worthy of it.

Charles Hicks

[April 1813] On Good Friday, *the 16th* . . . After this service everyone, young and old, went in silent order to our barn, which had been prepared in the best way possible for the baptism of our Charles Hicks. At the beginning, a Passion song was sung and then an appropriate talk to everyone gathered. Finally, with great seriousness and emphasis directed to our pupils, we explained their responsibility toward Him, Who created them and bought them with the pains of His death to be His own. . . .

After a fervent prayer, Brother Gambold carried out the baptism accompanied by a breeze of the peace of our crucified Lord; this cannot be described. Everyone broke down in tears, dedicated himself, consecrated the one being baptized, who is to us so worthy of Him, the good Lord, and to His service forever. He received the name Charles Renatus.[21] Then we knelt down, and he fell, as well as he could since he has one lame leg[22] and has to use a crutch, on his face and with wet eyes worshipped His great patron, Lord and God.

His well-mannered but otherwise still completely *Indian* wife[23] also had eyes full of tears. Joseph Crutchfield,[24] who had never before attended such an event, cried unceasingly, as did our Alice.[25] After those gathered had dispersed, we asked Mrs. Hicks if she had not also felt something special inside. She said in broken English, "Yes, I believe I did."[26]

Our baptized one was very sorry, as we also were that some of his Indian friends and relatives, whom he had invited three weeks ago, were kept from coming by the streams, which were made impassable by the high waters. We later heard that The Ridge, who had set out on the way with his daughter Nancy,[27] our former pupil, had to turn around at the water, and Nancy was completely inconsolable about this.

We were especially thankful that we were not at all disturbed by our wicked neighbor[28] on this festival day although the administrator Jim Brown[29] had arrived, and our Joseph Crutchfield was summoned. He was not happy to go, and our good Charles had Brown told through him that he asked them to spare Joseph. If he had something to bring up, have it rather brought to him. He was willing to speak with him in the evening or the next morning. However, Brown did not want to hear anything of this, but treated the distressed silent Joseph in the most condescending manner, repeated his threats about the field, and in other ways.[30] Upon his return Joseph looked very sad, and Peggy cried about the wrongful treatment of her husband. We comforted both of them; we asked them also to lay *this* unpleasant matter, which came from the evil enemy, at the feet of *Him*, Who had defeated him through His Crucifixion.

After the following service, both of them assured us that they had been indescribably comforted and added: "Oh the Lord is good."[31] Some of Peggy's relatives, who were traveling by, paid us a cordial visit at noon and ate with us but hurried on soon. In the evening we read the brief story of the burial; then sang to the beautiful corpse of Jesus and concluded in this way the certainly unforgettable Good Friday about which we must testify, "It was a day which the Lord made!"

James Vann's Rejection of Christianity

[June 1805] At three o'clock in the morning *on the 6th*, Mr. Vann sent for us and asked Brother and Sister Byhan[32] to visit him. Sister Byhan could not go for certain reasons, so Brother Byhan went alone. When he arrived there, he found Mr. Vann almost out of his mind with pain because a live creature had gotten into his ear. He himself believed he would pass away on this occasion. When Brother Byhan observed that he was thinking about death and seemed to be very uneasy about it, he directed him to the Friend of poor sinners and told him that the Savior came into this world for him as well, poured out His blood for him, and died for him. If he believes in Him now, He will accept him into grace. In answer to the question of whether he believed then that the Savior poured out His blood and died for *him*, he answered, No!—he did not believe. He did not believe that there was a Jesus Christ; all such things like that were imagined. After a while, when the creature came out of his ear and he did not have any more pain, he began talking then on his own about the fact that he did not believe that there was a Jesus Christ.

Annuity Distribution at Vann's Plantation

The United States government paid annuities in exchange for land ceded in treaties. Anna Rosina described a few of the annuity distributions that took place between 1805 and 1821 in the following treaties the U.S. Senate ratified and the presidents signed: the Third Treaty of Tellico, October 25, 1805; the Fourth Treaty of Tellico (which allowed for a mail route through the Cherokee and Creek nations), October 27, 1805; the First Treaty of Washington,

January 7, 1806; the Second Treaty of Washington, March 22, 1816; the Third Treaty of Washington, March 22, 1816; the Treaty of the Chickasaw Council House, September 14, 1816; the Treaty of the Cherokee Agency, July 8, 1817; and the Fourth Treaty of Washington, February 27, 1819, concluded March 1, 1819.[33]

[October 1806] *On Sunday the 5th* . . . Our Indian children also have a serious lack of clothing, and we have already helped them almost past our means. He[34] *promised* his help regarding both issues, especially because soon the annuities would be distributed to the Indians. At that time he would remember our children as well since it is right and proper that we should also be helped in such difficulties.

Unfortunately this good intention will probably remain unfulfilled because this distribution will not take place this fall, but rather will occur next spring.[35]

[October 1807] Early in the day *on the 23rd*, our friend Chuleoa[36] came with his wife and one of his daughters; we made them breakfast. Soon afterward we received a friendly visit from Chief Kotoquaski,[37] William Hicks,[38] and Corn Silk. The latter, who is a relative of our Tommy,[39] gave the school a present, a bundle of quill pens. All three looked at the children's writing books. In the afternoon we went to visit the camps in two groups, because we could not all be gone from the house at the same time on account of the work and the many strangers. The camps stretched from our field to Hall's[40] and from there up to the Conasauga, and on the other side from our place up to Josiah Vann's.[41]

Around Vann's house it was teeming with people. Soon afterward Alexander Saunders,[42] The Ridge,[43] and Charles McDonald,[44] our Johnston's[45] father, came into the Byhans' house with a small barrel of whiskey and asked for a tin drinking cup; they served the whiskey and drank until they were all completely drunk. Still, they asked the Byhans not to be afraid, because no harm would come to them. Soon afterward Saunders and The Ridge left.

But Charles McDonald, who neither could stand nor walk, laid himself down against our garden fence and fell asleep. His elder son, as well as young Johnston, who seemed to act out of childlike love and devotion, helped him afterward in the twilight onto his horse and took him away. He himself seemed to be ashamed of his behavior in front of us later. Old Chiquaki[46] did the same. Since his last wild entrance, he keeps quite withdrawn in the schoolhouse. If you want to talk with him he casts his eyes down in embarrassment.

At this opportunity we noticed that at least one of the sober Indians always stays with a drunk one and guards him until he is peaceful again. Also the former tries to put his knife and weapons off to the side for the time being so that nothing bad happens. Thus an elderly man, who was lodging in our kitchen with his wife, gave Brother Byhan his knife with the request to keep it until the drunken ones were gone. . . .

. . . The air in recent days has been so full of smoke that we can hardly recognize anything around our houses and cannot even recognize them from a short distance, especially in the morning and evening. Indeed the smoke filled the air so much that it was extremely unpleasant and one became hoarse from it.

In addition to that was the constant running back and forth of the Indians. Because of the bringing and fetching of their horses from our field, the fences were always left open so that our cattle, cows, calves, horses, and pigs all came into our courtyard and close to the houses. When we wanted to drive them away in the morning, we could not see them because of the smoke.

None of us had ever experienced such thick smoke in the air! The many campfires, which looked really magnificent in the night, may also have contributed to the woods actually catching on fire here and there, because we have had mostly dry weather for a long time; all the growth was dried out and this added to the thick smoke.

[October 24, 1807] . . . In the afternoon, as our Indians had also gone there, we all went to Vann's because we had learned that the chiefs there would hold talks. Now, we never expected to find such a crowd of people there, because only the Upper Cherokees had been called here. There are supposed to be between four and five hundred [thousand] old and young, men, women and children.

From Vann's house as far as the *eye* could see into the woods everything was full of ancient people, among whom were also white, half brown, and very dark colored, and a host of children! But there was such quiet and order that it amazed us! During our visit Chiefs Chuleoa and The Flea spoke alternately, and the gathering listened reverently. Occasionally one heard a "*Howago*!" (We are satisfied!) or *Osio!* (Good!)[47] from the side of the listeners.

Many were comically painted with black and red dots on their face and the same kind of rings around their eyes. Others had square black spots outlined with red on their cheeks and still others had red crosses above their noses and white rings around their eyes. Their dress was equally strange. We were very delighted to find some acquaintances among them; some greeted us quite cordially.

We commended our poor Indian children to our friend Mr. Charles Hicks, to remember them during the distribution. We had hardly been home half an hour when three Indians came to our place. One of them, a very good-looking young man, especially attracted our attention. He looked so pale that one feared he would sink to the ground. At his request Brother Petersen[48] fetched him water. However, the Indian did not wait for him to dip it, but rather bent over to the pail in Brother Petersen's hand and drank quickly from it after which he and his companions left for their camp. Not long afterward we learned that this young man had stolen horses and immediately after we had left Vann's was bound to a tree and received one hundred lashes, which were given to him by twenty head men. . . .

This evening some drunken Indians made a horrible noise near our houses. Among these was one of Chuleoa's sons, who acted very funny and sang dance songs. Their companions soon tried to get them away and into the camps, so that we could sleep peacefully.

[October 25, 1807] . . . Last night and this morning, as Mr. Vann had four heads of cattle slaughtered at public cost, including one for his family, our good old Jenny[49] went there quietly and fetched as much as she could carry. We thanked her sincerely for this as we have not had meat since we have had so many guests neither for them nor for our own table. Now, however, we all got a good meal.

Afterward we received a little bit more from Mrs. Vann,[50] who had gotten hardly any for her own family, because the many half-starved

Indians had grabbed it greedily, when it was hung up, and carried away as much as they could. Brother Gambold went to Vann's very early to be on hand so that our children would not be forgotten at the distribution. He was lucky enough to get a scarf and cotton for a jacket for each one, for which he thanked Mr. Charles Hicks especially sincerely.

Since we could not hold any services because of the overflow of people today, we all finally went to Vann's to watch the distribution a little. Upon our arrival we were astonished to see the Indian who was so horribly whipped yesterday standing on Vann's porch, happy and in good shape, joking with his comrades.

During the distribution of the annual gifts, everything proceeded quietly and orderly. Each town delivered as many little pieces of wood bound together to denote the people they had to the chiefs, who then carried out the distribution; they gathered above in Vann's house. Linen or wool cloth, scarves, and such things were bound in bundles. After the translator, who stood outside in front of Vann's window in the second floor on a board put there for that purpose, called the name of the town or district, one of the head people, who lives there, ran up and grabbed the bundle, which the caller extended outwardly. After he received it, everyone for whom it was intended followed him silently into the distance.

Some of the bundles had brass kettles along with knives and combs. Nevertheless, the personal distribution took place very inequitably, as we later learned from some of the Indians. Some of them receive just a couple of strips of flannel to tie their boots together; another receives a comb; yet others receive blankets, or things of similar value. Most of them do not complain, but rather seem satisfied.

Unfortunately, however, we see examples of some that feel offended. For example, one woman stood in our kitchen with her young girl and cried bitterly that she did not receive a blanket. Her old mother said that she should, therefore, complain to Colonel Meigs, from whom the Lower Cherokees would yet receive their annuity; she immediately set out on the road there.

The Indians receive this annuity from the government of the United States, because of the land that they ceded to them. To our delight we learned from their chiefs that such a distribution to the nation will not take place in the future, but rather the entire nation will receive the annuity from the agent.

[October 1807] *On the 26th* a northwesterly wind blew up, and the air became lighter; we were very happy about this. Many Indians were still staying at our place, and our George's mother[51] just arrived here this morning. She seemed very happy when we told her that her son's behavior was a joy to all of us here. One of old mother Vann's aunts visited us as well. She seems to be quite well on in years, but of a very lively nature. She spent the night.

Chief Bark[52] and another Indian visited the school. We took the latter in for the midday meal. To her and our delight, our good old Jenny, who had received nothing from the annuity after waiting for such a long time, received a blanket today through the petition of Chief Bark, who is her relative and in whose house she lives. In the afternoon George's mother also left. . . .

Probably several hundred Indians, who have stayed in our neighborhood during this time, have suffered from hunger. We gave everyone who asked for it something and those who asked came unceasingly day after day. However, how happy and thankful we were to our good Lord, who arranged it so that our dear Brethren[53] had to return to Springplace and were able to work with us during this busy time! Most importantly they, along with Brother Byhan, could bring our Indian corn and sweet potatoes in safely before the many Indians arrived; much of Mr. Vann's corn and *all* of his sweet potatoes were stolen from his field.

In the evening Chuleoa came with his family and spent the night with us, and *on the 27th*, after breakfast, they set off on their trip home, as well as old Jenny, to whom we were greatly indebted for her many faithful services to us during this busy time. We also gave her a pair of woolen socks as a sign of our gratitude. We saw it as a merciful act of God that this person was the first of the Indians, who came to us at this time. She seemed to fit right in with our ways and remained faithfully by us to turn away other Indians, who requested more from us than we could give. She also attended all of our services with reverence. . . .

[October 12, 1815] . . . After the noonday meal Dawzizi[54] proceeded with his father to the agency in order to receive distribution of the annuity[55] and a few necessary items. Brother Gambold commended him in a written way to Colonel Meigs.

[November 8, 1815] . . . In the evening The Tyger arrived again from the agency[56] with his son Dawzizi. The latter was very pleased to be with us again. He could not attain his goal at Colonel Meigs's in part because of his son's death[57] but also because of the obtrusiveness of so many white creditors, who had made claims against the Indians.[58] The agent could not satisfy them further[59] and a great quarrel occurred. Certainly the upstanding, kindhearted man is to be lamented.

We sighed to our dear Lord on his account. Dawzizi could not really find enough words to describe the godless desolation, mainly perpetrated by the many white people gathered there. There was to have been nine thousand people gathered.

[November 13, 1815] . . . [Charles Hicks] could not express enough his gratefulness for the dear Savior that in the midst of the wretched annuity turmoil, he found peace. The godless whites and also many proceedings at the agency went beyond all words to respected half-breeds. They complained also to dear saddened Colonel Meigs. Our Brother repeated that he was heartily encouraged by his orders and wished for *quietness*, because his efforts for the preservation of the nation had to be attained.

Cherokee Education, Moravian Style

"My dear Parents are both ignorant of the English Language, but it is astonishing to see them exert all their power to have their Children educated like the whites," wrote John Ridge to President James Monroe in 1821.[60] According to historian and scholar of Cherokee culture, the late William G. McLoughlin, Cherokees historically were achievement oriented, which enticed young and old warriors to measure their status by displaying daring deeds in war and hunting—through the quantity of scalps, captives, or furs and hides that they collected. Edified in songs and dances, their exploits had revealed their heroism and restored sense of pride. Yet these outward signs of achievement were also measures of a Cherokee male's importance to his family, clan, and tribe; they were visible signs of his attaining harmony with the spirits that controlled life.[61]

After 1790, however, Cherokees were expected to exchange their warrior image for book learning. The Treaty of 1791 stipulated that in order for the

Cherokee Nation to gain a greater degree of civilization they were to become herdsmen and cultivators, instead of remaining hunters. "If they acquiesced the United States will, from time to time, furnish, gratuitously, the said nation with useful implements of husbandry."[62] *As Cherokees expected Springplace to deliver the "arts of civilization," Anna Rosina anticipated that the pupils along with their parents would obey scholastic and moral strictness, the opportunities present in a "civilized" society.*[63] *That entailed the learning of English and becoming a time-oriented society. Most of the pedagogical experiences at the Springplace mission school went unreported. Headmistress Anna Rosina used the Lancasterian system, the educational practices of British Quaker and charity school reformer Joseph Lancaster (1778–1838). Older pupils and more advanced pupils, or "monitors," instructed the younger ones, providing Anna Rosina with a disciplinary approach to schooling.*[64] *This competitively based, achievement-oriented classroom gave Anna Rosina the necessary pedagogical approaches she needed to instruct Cherokee sons and daughters.*[65] *Additionally, Lancasterian methodology focused on utilitarian, meritocratic, and moralistic purposes, instilling ways that Cherokee youth could embrace the socially accepted republican way of life. Cherokee youth relied on rote memory, another Lancasterian method, reinforcing the spelling of words and memorizing math formulas and geographical locations.*[66]

Whether Cherokee parents approved of the Lancasterian method remains uncertain. What is known, however, was that pupils had many opportunities to voice their complaints among themselves about the missionaries' treatment of them, and such complaints to Cherokee relatives gave rise to multiple misunderstandings, intensifying conflicts between parents and missionaries. Even infractions of Moravian rules, however slight, exacerbated Cherokee distrust for the missionaries. While the very nature of offenses went unrecorded, punishment or dismissal was the norm.

Children's Illnesses at the Mission
Dick and Johnny

[September 1809] Early in the day *on Sunday the 24th* . . . Our two Indian boys, Johnny[67] and Dick,[68] who got a fever at the beginning of last week, could not attend the sermon. In the evening Dick's brother, named The Young Bird, came to visit and he spent the night.

On the 28th The Young Bird came with two horses to take Dick home because, as he said, we did not have any doctors here. Dick, who was in bed with a very high fever, cried loudly when we informed him of his brother's intentions. Then we asked Mrs. Vann to come to our house and had her speak with the child in *their* language in the presence of his brother, so that no misunderstanding would occur. We would be blamed for this as if we had kept the child from his parents. Anyway, on account of the children, we were constantly wavering between fear and hope, since their recovery still seemed to be very far away. The illness increased from day to day, and it appeared ever more evident that it was a very bad strong fever. In answer to Mrs. Vann's question to Dick about whether he wanted to go with his brother or not, he immediately answered with a "no." Crying, he hid his face with his blanket. None of us said a word, but we were happy and thankful that it turned out *this* way since the poor boy could not possibly have stood a ride of twenty miles[69] on a very bad road. Besides this it would certainly have been very painful for us to deliver him into heathen hands, since he and Johnny, much to our delight, have recently given clear indications that they set their faith in the dear Savior and clearly believe He will treat them according to His love.

So The Young Bird left early *on the 29th*. At noon a well-known Indian from Rabbit Trap came in order to attend our evening service, as he said. We were very sorry that we had to let him know through our Alice Shorey[70] that we could not hold a service *this* evening because of our children's illness. Particularly Johnny had been so weakened by a nosebleed, which he came down with several evenings ago and which continued until midnight, that he could neither stand nor walk without help. We had to support him continually. We provided the visiting Indian with hospitality as well as we could. We made him a fire and a place to sleep in the schoolhouse, because the Gambolds had taken the sick children into their house at the beginning of this week, and we had a comforting heart-to-heart talk with him. We encouraged him to visit us again soon, because we would hopefully then have an opportunity to grant his requests. He took this very well and promised to come again soon.

[October 1809] To our delight *on the 4th*, Dick's grandfather The Flea arrived here. He had heard about his grandson's illness, and at the same time heard the most shameful lies from the mouth of The Young Bird, who, as it now seemed, was angry that his brother was unwilling to go home with him. Thus he had pretended that we had not let him in the house, that he had not been allowed to see his brother, and that it was only *our* fault that he did not go home with him, and so on. The Flea said he had not believed him, because he knows us *better*. Mrs. Vann, to whom he had spoken several days ago at Mr. Charles Hicks's, had told him just the opposite. He also asked us not to take the matter to heart, as The Young Bird was a fool and a brazen liar, and no one who knew him paid the least attention to his words.

In the morning *on the 5th*, The Flea went out to look for some roots,[71] which should serve as an emetic for the sick children. Toward evening he returned and said that he had to go very far before he found any.

On Sunday the 8th, we could not have a service because of the sick children. At The Flea's request, we held a small *Singstunde* this evening. Then this dear man left us *on the 9th* again with the promise to come again as soon as possible. He repeatedly assured us that he always had a good feeling in his heart when he was in our midst and also that he was very satisfied with our treatment of the sick children. Everything that we were doing for the recovery of their health was right and good. He also asked for some roots from our medicinal herbs, which we were happy to give him.

On the 10th Dick's brother The Young Bird came again, but did not stay at our place long, just as his father[72] did *on the 11th*. He seemed very happy to find his son much better than he had imagined. Both of the children have really been well on the way to recovery since last Sunday so that we ourselves, after many troubled days, can hope for the recovery of their health in the near future.

In the morning *on Sunday the 15th*, Brother Byhan held a *Singstunde*. In the afternoon, since Dick has had a strong attack of fever again and no guests came for the service, we cancelled it. In the evening, a well-known Indian from Oostanaula came and asked for lodgings here, so our Johnny asked to go with him into the schoolhouse and sleep there; this was fine with us. We also had reason to believe that the fever has left him completely.

On the 18th as our Dickey was overcome with great weakness, he spent the whole day sleeping. He did not want to eat or drink anything, so that we were very worried about him. Our dear Lord arranged it so that toward evening, to our great encouragement, our friend The Flea arrived at our place again. He showed us his delight that his grandson had lost his fever and added that he was not at all worried about him; one could certainly not suddenly become strong again after a difficult illness.

John Ridge

[August 1811] *On the 6th* . . . Our John[73] has had a sore eye, which appears serious to us and has not improved despite all the means we have used, so we asked Peggy, whose youngest sister Charlotte[74] had just endured a lot with her eye for a long time so much so that we sometimes feared she would lose her sight in it, to take John into her house with her.

We believed he would more likely improve if he were distanced from his companions and could be kept under more careful watch in the house, and the parents would more likely be satisfied about the means used if they found the child with Peggy, as a member of their nation, than with us. We expect them for a visit any day. Because of a lack of language, we are not in a position to properly answer for him. She proved to be very willing to perform this service for us and promised to take care of the child as well as she could.

Young Buck,[75] a cousin of John, got the illness first. However, we were fortunate enough to cure him in a few days. It is indescribable how many sighs to the dear Savior are caused by such a circumstance in a country where one is completely without human help and cannot always hope for the best interpretation from the Indians should a child, even if not our fault, really becomes harmed.

[August 1811] *On the 12th* The Ridge and his wife[76] arrived here. The latter began to cry as soon as she entered into the house. At the ball play in Hightower, she had heard the horrible description of the sore eye of her John and the comment that she, during her stay here, would probably find him *one-eyed.* The mother could not describe how much she had feared on the way here the sight of her son, whose eye was dreadfully described to her. Oh, it cannot be said how very busy the father of lies, horrifying and presenting everything in the worst way, is in this country. And how many emissaries he has! Peggy and we have experienced this in innumerable ways, so that we do not believe much of what is told to us about events in the nation.

Oh, how happy both parents were when they learned from us that things with their child's eye were not nearly so bad. They also seemed very satisfied with what we had done for him, and after they had eaten, they went, reassured, to Peggy's to see the child for themselves. . . .

The festival *on the 13th* . . . Early in the day, we received visits, including The Ridge and his wife, who now seemed to be comforted about their son but had decided to carry him home and to take him to be treated by an old woman in their neighborhood. . . .

On the 14th The Ridge and his wife began their journey home with their John, but promised to bring him back as soon as he was cured.

[September 15, 1811] . . . In the evening Watie arrived here. He expressed his joy at the behavior of his children, Buck and Dawnee. He also delighted us with the news that the eye of his nephew John, The Ridge's son, has noticeably improved, and we could expect him here soon.

Pelican and Two Others

[May 1821] *On the 19th* The Tyger came to take his son Pelican home for a number of weeks. Three of our pupils scared us more than a little today. They had been in the woods and all of a sudden came running home crying and screaming and complained about strong pains in their bodies. In the first panic, we thought they had perhaps eaten poison, and thus gave them tree oil, which soon made them vomit. Then it turned out that they had eaten too much of the flower tops of honeysuckle or peonies,[77] which grow here in great numbers and have an unpleasant sour taste. After they vomited, the pains subsided. After they had drunk a bitter tea that our old Negro woman Pleasant[78] made for them, they were completely fit and well. However, we thought it would be good completely to prohibit them these delicacies in the future.

Removal of Children from the Mission School
Robert and Moses Parris

[December 1806] *On the 27th* we felled some wood for the construction of a spacious beehive, since our bees increased considerably last year. Turkey Cock and Dully[79] offered to fetch the beams for us, which we gladly agreed to. Toward evening Moses and Robert[80] Parris came to tell us goodbye, because their father has arrived at Vann's to take them home.

We thought they just meant for a visit when *on Sunday the 28th*, they came to us again early in the day in the company of a sixteen-year-old young man and indicated to us that their father wanted to take them home to stay; the young man would be their schoolmaster. The latter then pulled out a small monkey, which he had on a chain under his coat, to amuse the children. Once again Moses and Robert departed from us very congenially. In the presence of their new teacher, we gave them a number of useful exhortations. One could clearly see that they were not happy about going. Brother Gambold then went to Vann's to see and speak with Mr. Parris once more. He told him that it hurt him as well to withdraw his children from our instruction. However, since he has had to listen to repeated complaints from Mr. Vann about their behavior in his house, and since on his journey to Tellico he found this young man who was raised in the state of Tennessee, he thought that it would be better to take his children home in order to have them under his own supervision. At least he wanted to test the young man's skill in instructing the children. We could not say anything against this. However, it really hurt us. These children had gotten quite used to things at our place and had learned to behave by our rules. Not only had they behaved themselves quite *well* in school and studied diligently but also the elder one could already read fairly well and the younger one, who did not understand a word of English when he entered our school, was also beginning to read. We also especially noticed, however, that they were not only attentive to what they were told about God and godly things, but they also *liked* to listen.

During the Christmas holidays, they were unusually happy and did not miss any of the services. They had also learned many Christmas and other verses with the other children. Just a few days ago, Moses asked our children if *God could read.* They answered, "Yes, He certainly could, and not only that, but He can understand you when you talk very *leichte*, easy, meaning softly, with Him." Moses was amazed at this and asked for further explanation, which we very gladly gave him.

After Mr. Parris ate breakfast at Vann's, he left with the young schoolmaster, his two sons, and a barrel full of whiskey, to catch up on *Christmas.*

Tommy, son of Gentleman Tom or Chuleoa

[September 1806] *Early on the 12th,* Gentleman Tom came here for breakfast. Afterward he asked for various kinds of garden seeds, which we gladly gave him. We were very happy to hear that the potatoes, which he got from us in the spring, had produced well. He also informed us that he was planning to take his Tommy home for a visit,[81] where he will supervise him well, and bring him back in a couple of weeks. Although we were not very happy to let the child go, nevertheless, we certainly could not refuse his father.

[August 20, 1808] . . . Toward noon Chuleoa also arrived here with his wife in order to take Tommy home for the Green Corn Dance,[82] an annual communal celebration in this nation; it must not be confused with the private dance in families before the *first* new corn is eaten. We also let these good people know through Mrs. Vann that we were not happy to see this, because the boy might get into excesses and get completely out of his school routine.

This was taken very *well,* and they promised us they would watch him as well as possible and also would bring him back in ten days. His stepmother told us in confidence that Tommy himself had asked his father some time ago to get him for the dance. This news troubled us greatly.

Moreover, Chuleoa was very friendly toward us as usual. He also told us that he had been at Colonel Hawkins's[83] some weeks ago, but had met him a day's journey away from our Brethren,[84] whom he would also like to have seen. Because of his companion's illness, he was prevented from doing so. Very early in the day, these dear guests left with Tommy.

[August 1809] *On the 24th* Chuleoa wanted to take his son Tommy home for several weeks. Early in the day, Brother and Sister Gambold went with him to Mrs. Vann so that we could tell him through her that we were not very happy about the children making such visits home, because they not only are set back in their learning, but also get completely out of the school routine. He took this *very well*, but said that he really needs Tommy for several weeks since he has livestock to look for in the woods, and his other sons, who are already grown, do not want to help him because they are too lazy.

He said he would supervise him well and not let him be in the company of George Vann,[85] who lives only five miles from him, because George has already spread several lies about us. For example, the children here did not get enough to eat, and when they were sick, they were not taken care of, and so on. However, he knows that these are lies, because he knows us better. Then he then promised to bring him back in three or four weeks.

Tawoadi, son of Suakie

[April 1808] In the morning *on the 8th*, a very respectable Indian, also named Suakie,[86] came and brought his young son Tawoadi,[87] Great Hawk, to the school. The child will live at the Vann's.

[June 1809] Early in the day *on the 27th*, Suakie came and informed us that he wanted to take his son Tawoadi home with him for a visit and expressed his displeasure that his boy plays with Negro children so much. It is his desire that he constantly have his book in front of him and learn. Despite this, in answer to our question about how long he would keep him away from school, he answered, "*As long as Tawoady wants*"!!

Alice Shorey

[July 1809] In the morning *of the 22nd*, Mother Vann and Mrs. Vann came here with Mrs. McDonald[88] and her niece, Alice Shorey. The latter was enrolled with us as a pupil last year by her uncle, Mr. John McDonald.[89] Family circumstances, however, prevented her coming before now. Mrs. McDonald was very happy to have reached her goal, because she had promised her brother, Chief William Shorey, before his death that she would arrange a good education for his two daughters.

Therefore, she also expressed her wish to have the younger daughter Lydia in our hands, but added that she hardly knew how she would get her out of the hands of their relatives,[90] who had taken her away from her through deception. We told her that we would be glad to serve her by taking on the care of this child as well, but that at the present time we did not have room to take her in.

[April 21, 1810] . . . In the evening Mr. John Ross[91] arrived here with a letter from Mrs. McDonald in which she asked us to let her niece Alice Shorey go home for a visit, as she *herself* would like to have visited us for Easter, but was prevented from doing so by gout pain. She promised to bring the child back to us herself as soon as her health allowed it. We were all very sorry to see this dear, promising girl leave here even for a short time. It was very painful, however, for *her*, and she cried the whole night. At our persuasion, and in the hope of being back with us soon, she left here early *on the 23rd* with Mr. Ross, her relative.

[June 1810] *On the 19th* . . . Toward evening our friend Mr. John McDonald arrived with his wife's niece Alice Shorey, who was visiting at her aunt's house.

[April 1811] Toward evening *on the 16th*, Mr. John McDonald arrived here. He came to take home his wife's niece, our dear girl Alice Shorey. This was unpleasant news for her and for us, since she now feels completely at home here. She had also received a true gift in the Word of God, so that her favorite activity was to copy the most powerful, especially the Passion songs from the hymnal, and she also found her greatest pleasure in singing.

Early in the day *on the 17th*, she left us and there were many tears on both sides.

John Gonstadi

[April 1815] *On the 5th* in the evening, Qualiyuga, the mother of our little Jack, or Gonstadi,[92] attended our service. We read out of the *Harmony of the Four Gospels*.[93]

In the afternoon *on the 6th*, the visitor returned home. At her request we had to send her little son with her, as she said, because he had an ailment in his chest since childhood. Yet the child and we were unaware of it. For certain there was no noticeable sign of it. She asserted that the grandmother wanted to cure the child. The child cried bitterly and did not want to follow her. Only through all sorts of promises, including that she would bring him back in ten days, did the child finally give in.

Oh, the great passion of the evil enemy! Be gone! In its grip, it disturbs the entire being of our children. We sighed and commended the needy little one truly earnestly to the dear Savior for safekeeping.

Buck Watie and John Ridge

[April 11, 1815] . . . In the afternoon The Ridge and Watie arrived here in order to take their sons home to have them taught by a white man. They had hired him for the purpose of tutoring their children.[94] It is generally well known to us that this type of white people is forced upon the unwitting Indians for such services. So at this time it was with our poor children, in this particular case of the son of Watie, our little hopeful, Buck. The Ridge requested to speak with us. We let our Peggy attempt to find the purpose, which she also did. Through her we let The Ridge say to us that he was very thankful for all our efforts we had given his son. He wanted to take him home to a white man whom he insisted would bestow instruction all year long. He will always gratefully recognize our efforts with his son and consider that he owes his knowledge above all to us.

Yet he himself scarcely thought that his new teacher was prepared to impart *the* instruction to him compared to what he had received here, etc. So Brother Gambold acknowledged to him that he might easily find a white man in the nation who could qualify as a teacher of our children in reading and writing and also impart skill; however, we fully know to instruct the same. However, *our* main work in the children's education was to make them know their Creator and Redeemer.

Then their temporal and eternal welfare as well would lie on our hearts also. It caused us deep pain when children were torn away from our care and were entrusted to such people, whose moral conduct caused pain to our God and was of greatest harm to our needy children. Our Peggy repeated this speech devotedly, especially the powerful addition leading from her own heart. The Ridge understood everything as the *truth* and *good words*. He remained resolved, however, together with his brother, to take the children, as this was the design, and to entrust the children to his new teacher; they *hoped* he was a *good* man. He assured this often by repeating that he would remain our friend for all times. Poor little Buck aroused our dear compassion. With extended hands and loud crying, he begged his father to nevertheless let him stay with us, but to no avail. His father went with him step-by-step and expressively asked that he be intent on leaving.

He also promised that if the new teacher should not be favored, he could bring him to us again. So our greatest protests went late into the night as we certainly made use of our distinctive stirrings often of the merciful work of our Holy Spirit in the heart of our poor child.

On the 12th they rode away after breakfast. John, The Ridge's son, was really confident, indeed, joyful. On the contrary, Buck was crying and sighing. We cried out to him, "God bless and protect you, my child." After the departure, he was still crying. Everyone proceeded into the quiet as we commended this poor child quite urgently to the Protector of Mankind. What our needy souls felt during this tearful event is indescribable.

Rumors of Mistreatment of Students

[August 1809] *On the 28th* Chiquaki came to see for himself, as he said, if what George Vann had been saying at Pine Log, that our school had been dissolved and the children who were still there were only being fed *once* a day. If this were the case, he would take his Johnny home. He was very happy to find that matters here were continuing in the usual way. In a very friendly way, he let us know through the children that the Indians had lent us some of their land so that we could work it to nourish some of their children and ourselves from it!

Runaway Students

Iskittihi

[January 1806] *On Sunday the 26th* . . . Iskittihi[95] left silently with all of the clothing that belonged to him and went to his people. As sorry as we were to *lose* him, the most capable of our students at the time, we were also happy that we were rid of a tempter of the others. He had proven himself to be such since he came back from his people without our permission.

Tlaneneh

[September 1809] *On the 6th* Suakee,[96] an Indian who is very well disposed toward us, visited us and asked if we would take in his young son to rear.

A place was available for this child because of George's departure from us, but we did not want to promise him anything before we had considered this together. Thus Brother Gambold advised him to come back in a couple of weeks, and he would then be answered. . . .

On the 7th . . . During a small lovefeast,[97] we considered the request made by Suakee yesterday.

Since Brother Gambold had already spoken with Mrs. Vann about the matter and had learned from her that this Indian truly had the character of an honest man, we decided that when he returned we would tell him that we would take him in, if he could assure us that we would not receive visits from his child's harmful relatives. His wife's[98] family has a very bad reputation.

[September 30, 1809] . . . . In the afternoon Suakee came and brought his young boy named Tlaneneh for us to care for. He said that the child was seven years old. In accordance with our decision several days ago when he came here for an answer, we had let him know our wish, through Mr. Charles Hicks, that his wicked relatives should stay away from him. As he himself said, this was absolutely what he intended since he does not want his child to have any association with them.

[October 1809] *On the 19th* Suakee also came to see his young son and was very happy to see him so well.

[May 31, 1810] In the afternoon Suakee came to visit us with his wife and children, and they proved to be unusually friendly. He was very happy to find thatı his young Tlaneneh[99] had already begun *reading*. In a way in which no Indian has expressed himself to us before, he thanked us for our efforts with him. He added that it was his wish that we would keep him in our care for quite a long time; we truly and happily promised to do so. Since he had not completely recovered his own health, he asked again for some herbs. We were happy to serve him with these.

[February 1811] Early in the day before school *on the 13th*, when the boy Tlaneneh was spoken to about something, this annoyed him so much that he silently got his things together and went with them to his parents.

[March 1811] *On Sunday the 24th* . . . In the afternoon the brother of our friend Suakee, who is ill, came and asked for some corn for the sick man. We gave it to him as well as a quantity of dry beans. This was the first time since Tlaneneh ran away from us that anyone from his father's family has let himself be seen here. We took advantage of this opportunity to ask about the boy and his behavior at his relatives' place. The good man believed we had sent him home. Thus it was strange to him that he learned he had left here without our knowledge.

He had us told through Jack Still[100] that the sick father knows nothing else but that we allowed his son to go home on a visit and to stay there until the famine was over. We cannot tell if the boy, who does not yet completely understand English, so misunderstood our talk or whether he thought up this untruth so that he could go his own way at least for a time. In the meantime we let the father know the truth about the matter and assured him that we certainly would not send any of our children home because of the lean times. It was also our rule not to take back any child who had run away from our school. Nonetheless, considering that Tlaneneh was still young and not able to reason, we would, perhaps, make an exception for the sake of the father, whose child's education means so much and whose illness prevents him from keeping an eye on him. He promised to report this faithfully.

[May 1811] *On the 25th* our former pupil Tlaneneh's mother and her sister came and said that the boy now wanted to come to our school again. We replied that it was against our rules to take back runaway pupils.

[October 1811] *On the 7th* . . . Our runaway pupil Tlaneneh's mother asked us to take her son into the school again, because he really desires this. However, we refused flatly with the explanation that this would be a bad example for the others and could not be tolerated at all. She replied that it was amazing that we only kept the children for such a short time. Then we had her told that we would like to have kept her son for quite a long time here, but he had left secretly. Because of this, we could not take him in again.

Rumors of Abductions

[April 1809] Early in the day *on the 1st,* Chiquaki set out on his journey home. This honest old Indian is fond of us and likes to hear his grandson Johnny talk about *God* and *good things.* Yet one cannot say at this time if there are signs that such words are making a *deep* impression on his heart. He had us told a story about an Indian from Pine Log,[101] where *he* lives. The Indian had gone out hunting in the mountains and seen many deer tracks. However, a voice very close by him cried out to him, "There are few deer this year!—and the man who lives in the clouds is angry at the Indians, because they are killing each other. When they have killed seven more, he will send *rain* and kill all the evil Indians and make it completely dark for four days."

On this occasion Chiquaki asked us if those who live in peace and did not kill anyone would also be killed. We spoke with him sincerely and advised him to remain in a childlike manner with Him, Who lives in heaven and Whose eyes see the deeds of all human children on the earth. . . . He also said that he came to see if the rumor, which he had heard at home, was *true*: "Our pupils had been picked up by the white people and would be taken into the settlements since Mr. Vann was no longer living." He would now leave us satisfied, because he had found out that this matter had absolutely no basis. It is indescribable how the father of lies is so busy in this country and how the Indians give him immediate approval.

Rumors of Hunger

[February 1811] At breakfast *on the 19th*, The Flea, who spent the night here with his family, told us that our Johnny and Johnston indicated to him that they wanted to leave us in a few days as Tlaneneh had done. He added that he would try to prevent them from this foolish intention. We replied that we would be very thankful to him for this and expressed to him our sorrow at Tlaneneh's behavior. He had not been here eighteen months and was a very capable child; we still hope that he will regret the step he took and return to us. The Flea kept his promise and spoke very seriously with the children, especially with his grandchild Dick.

When asked why they wanted to leave us, their answer was because they do not get enough to eat. The Flea, who left very quickly, had Alice Shorey tell this to Brother Gambold. This is fashionable with the Indians.

When children live with other people and want to go home, they only need to pretend that they are suffering from hunger, and they will be picked up immediately. The enemy would also like to use this means at our school as well. However, praise be to God, he did not succeed in it this time. We called all the children together right away to investigate this unpleasant matter. Dawzizi and John Ridge admitted that they had told The Flea that they were sometimes hungry after eating. Upon further investigation they said that when such things happened they had always had enough to eat at noon and in the evening, but at breakfast, it had sometimes happened that our Negro woman[102] had given them too little bread. We let them know how upsetting their behavior toward us was since we had so often repeated to them that if they did not have enough food, they only needed to come and tell us.

As often as they had done this, they always received more. We asked them why they had not told us if things were as they said instead of complaining to the Indians, who at the current time have much less to eat than they do. We received no answer to this, and some of them seemed to be very disturbed, so we let them go for the time being and did not hold school.

In the afternoon we asked Peggy to speak with them in their own language because some of them still do not completely understand the English language. She told them our thoughts about their behavior, and of her own accord, she reprimanded them sharply, telling them how much luckier they were than so many others in their nation to be raised by children of God and also to enjoy the best care in physical regards. She did this in so animated a manner that even those who appeared completely unemotional before seemed to be deeply moved. Yes, all of them broke out in loud crying. Now each one was asked individually if he wanted to leave us or to follow our rules and deal with us honestly.

Dawzizi said, "My father brought me here so that I would learn what is good and I do not want to leave." Johnston: "I really want to stay here longer, unless you no longer want to have me here." Dick: "My father told me that I should learn diligently here, and if I deserve it, then you should punish me." Johnny Gutseyedi could hardly speak for the tears, but also promised to improve. John, The Ridge's son, said, "I have not been here long at all and am just beginning to learn. My school time will be short enough. Why should I want to leave then?" The youngest, Buck, said smiling, "I am happy that people treat me well."

Now Brother Gambold talked to them emphatically again and asked them urgently not to throw away their greatest happiness intentionally.

Their temporal and eternal well-being depends on *how* they surrender, in their tender years, to the dear Savior, Who endured so much for them. . . . We really hope that this talk will remain meaningful and be a blessing to our miserable children.

Children's "Errant" Behavior

George Vann

[March 1807] In the morning *on the 5th* . . . A Negro woman[103] complained to Mrs. Vann today about our George, saying he had stolen thread from her weaving house. We were happy when the latter immediately let us know about the matter through her Mary.[104] In answer to our question as to whether he knew about the matter, he admitted that he had actually had the thread in his hands last Sunday when he was there without our knowledge. He had only looked at it and then put it down again right away. We advised him to go to Mrs. Vann immediately and to tell her the truth. After much persuasion he finally did so, accompanied by his friends. He then told Mrs. Vann, in the presence of the Negro woman, exactly what he had told us. However, the latter stuck to her claim, and indeed, *added* the manner in which he was supposed to have carried it away. Suddenly, George became aware of something under the blanket, which she had around her, that seemed to him like the lost thread. He went up, took hold of it, and pulled it out to the great astonishment of Mrs. Vann. Then we took the opportunity to ask him and the other children once again never to go into the neighborhood without our previous knowledge, and also to leave everything alone in strange houses. By the way, the matter was quite apropos, because we had just warned the children a few days ago not to go to Vann's for amusement without telling us, and had mentioned this among other reasons for their staying away, that the Negroes would like to take the opportunity to blame them for petty thievery that they themselves committed. This would get them into great trouble with Mr. Vann. Now they remembered this and promised anew to be obedient.

Robin

[May 1817] *On the 28th*, Dawnee, mother of our Robin,[105] came with her younger son[106] and pleaded with us to take him into our school. We gave her an answer: we could not grant her request at this time.

On the 29th the most unpleasant scene took place between Robin and his mother. This past winter she had sent him a pair of stockings; however, these were much too small for him. Now she wished them returned because she wanted enough yarn to knit bigger stockings. This request angered the boy, and he exerted such great power that he tore the stockings out of her hand. He sprang out of the house with them and wanted to run away with them. Sister Gambold was fortunate to approach him through the other children. Then she took the stockings from his hand and the mother appeared. Annoyed about it, he tore into two parts a neck scarf his mother had given him and hid it so that she could not demand it from him. He sprang with frenzy into the yard and announced finally to his mother that if she wanted to lay her hand on him, he would *fight* her. She stood crying and shaking in the yard. Buck, making use of the situation, tried to bring the irrational youth to his senses and tried to console his mother. He cried a lot, as he could not soon achieve results. Finally Sister Gambold pleaded with his mother to fetch Brother Gambold from the woods for help. He talked and she was satisfied. He only said to her that he wished she would not strike her son so hard! He would be sent to him later. Meanwhile Sister Gambold asked him to talk with Buck, who served as the interpreter. Nevertheless, as the boy was a little pliable and cried bitterly, he promised to apologize to his mother. Brother Gambold came here for this purpose and spoke to him with forceful words about the severity of his crime, and finally he persuaded him that he must apologize on his knees to his mother.

In the morning *on the 30th*, the poor, troubled mother came and asked would we forgive her son's rampant behavior or forget about it, which we promised her to do. She said: "I am ashamed of him, and I do not have the heart to come into your house." Finally, she called us to her, gave us her hand (we did the same), and she said, "It should *never* happen again."

Unfortunately the boy is really dead in his heart and is of a *cruel* nature. Even when he was back home, he responded violently to the smallest offense. A young Creek Indian undoubtedly would have been killed had another not come soon there and prevented it!

A Child's Death at the Mission

[September 23, 1811] . . . In the evening our Buck's parents arrived here along with his sister Dawnee and another younger sister.[107]

On the 24th we had a blessed and happy celebration with our fourteen children, twelve of whom belong to the Cherokee Nation, and four Indian guests. The eldest daughter of Watie, the father of our Buck, the above-mentioned Dawnee, about nine years old, received permission to stay here at the solemn request of her and her parents. "She has often cried about it! She really wants to live with you!" Her parents had this told us through Peggy. We then considered the matter in our Missions Conference and, especially since the father had already made a request concerning this child a long time ago, we found no reason to hurt these truly upstanding people with a negative answer.

[December 1811]: *On the 24th* for the Christmas Eve celebration thirty-two people gathered. Among these were Mr. William Hicks and his son George as well as our friend Watie's Negro named Thunder, with his master's little son Deckadocka,[108] a very appealing child, who felt at home with his brother Buck and sister Dawnee here.

[September 1812] *On the Sunday the 27th* . . . At noon we had the indescribable pain of seeing our Indian girl Dawnee suddenly depart. The day before she seemed to be completely healthy in the morning and was unusually fit. Toward noon she was overcome with vomiting, which did not seem to be of any real consequence to us, since last spring she had had a strong attack of this kind. She did not complain about any pain but did not want to eat anything. Immediately she had to throw up the little food that we talked her into, as well as everything that we gave her as medicine. She mostly preferred to be outside of the house, and we had difficulty talking her into staying inside. It was the same today. Toward noon her situation seemed to become more serious so we asked her to lie down in bed, which she did. However, while we were at [the] table, she sneaked out again. Sister Gambold went after her to bring her back, but found her dying.

We cannot describe how we felt during this. We surely did what we could to wake her out of the presumed unconsciousness, but her soul had departed from her body. What pained us the most about this was that we had not been able to prepare her for her end and direct her again in her last hours to the Savior. Thus there was nothing left for us to do but commend her departing soul with hot tears to the merciful heart of Jesus to be gracious to her for the sake of His blood, which was also shed for this heathen child.

She really had a lot of heathen vices, for which she often had to be punished. At the same time, she thought very well of herself and could tell you quite frankly, "I am good Dawnee." Then we then told her, "You are not, you have a very depraved and angry heart." Sometimes she would sometimes break out in loud crying. If one then further asked, "Do you also know who can make your evil heart good?" She answered, "Yes, the dear Savior." She really liked to sing verses, especially "Dearest Jesus, come to me and abide eternally,"[109] etc. Now the loving Savior, Who gladly puts up with the lowly faltering of children, will certainly have perceived in mercy the procrastination of this young heathen.

She was about eleven years old. Now we were concerned about how we should let her parents know about this painful event. Then an Indian, whom we know, happened to bring venison here. We asked him to act as the messenger of this sad news for pay, which he agreed to do, and we loaned him a horse for this.[110] . . .

Early in the day *on the 28th* . . . Toward noon the father also arrived here. For a heathen, however, he was very calm and reasonable, and among other things said, "If my child had been with me, she would also have died. You are not in any way responsible for her death, because I know how well you always treated her."

We then made a coffin for her and dressed the corpse, as well as our poverty allowed, and also decorated her with flowers. This really pleased her father. Then the children sang some verses beside the corpse, who had a very friendly appearance. Finally her mother also arrived. The old Vann woman,[111] who had gathered here along with numerous white, brown, and black people out of curiosity, hurried to meet her and began a really heathen wailing, which so intensified the pain of the poor mother that she was completely beside herself.

However, our Peggy took her by the hand and brought her to herself again in an evangelical way and told her among other things, "God,

Who gave you this child, has also taken her back again, and what He does is not only right and good but also always happens out of fatherly love. He certainly wanted to save your child from some distress on earth through this early death." After the burial place had been prepared on a nearby hill in the woods, the corpse was accompanied there by white, brown, and black people. There Brother Gambold, after a song was sung, gave an emphatic talk about the certainty of death but the uncertainly of the hour of death. He most urgently asked those present to take this death as an example, and indeed, to think about the salvation of their immortal souls while it still is today and to turn in faith to the crucified Jesus Christ, Who tasted death for everyone and Whose profit is appropriated by the poor sinner. He alone can free them from the fear of death and punishment.

After a fervent prayer, the corpse was lowered into the grave with our liturgy. Many tears were shed during this event, and we could believe that our poor children received a lasting impression in their hearts. Both parents behaved in a very upstanding way during this, and the mother only cried silent tears. Then our Peggy repeated to them the meaning of the speech in their language as well as she could.

They were very attentive during this, and with the most obliging comments, they expressed their gratitude for all the love we showed their child in life and death. The father said, "It was our intention to leave her with you until she became like Sister Gambold in everything. However, now that she is no more, will you not eventually take our next daughter,[112] who is still very young, in her place in your care?" Full of amazement at their faith, we very gladly agreed to this. Then they assured us of their continuing friendship, took leave lovingly, and left for home. Since they had not wanted to eat anything while they were here, we gave them some food to take along. They took their young son Buck along with them for a visit.

Use of Alcohol

The introduction of alcohol to the Cherokees wrought considerable stress throughout the Cherokee Nation in the Early Republic. Anna Rosina's observations reflected William G. McLoughlin's later analysis that some Cherokees turned to "spirituous liquor" to obliterate the loss and sense of anomie that Cherokees experienced during this time. The overwhelming presence of whiskey everywhere exacerbated that sense of despair.[113] *So pervasive was the problem that Anna Rosina recorded many incidents of Cherokees arriving at the mission inebriated and demanding food and shelter. She did not judge Cherokees inferior or defective because of alcohol abuse; rather, she displayed sympathy and concern for problems that families faced.*[114]

John McDonald

[June 1810] *On the 21st* after breakfast Mr. McDonald set off again on his journey home. . . .

He complained a lot about the bad things going on in the Cherokee Nation at the present time and the great influx into it of godless white people who are the greatest harm to the nation. He also told about various gruesome murders that Indians here and there in the country have recently committed against their own people and added that such things had never happened before during his forty years of living here, because drunkenness had not been so common.

The Ridge

[October 12, 1814] The Ridge said he had not seen us for a long time now and he was happy the whole way here that this pleasure was anticipated, and this joy increased the closer he came to our place. Then we told him what we had heard from upstanding people about the excesses of the Indians in Coosawattee and other places. We explained to him the danger that could arise for the nation from these, if peaceful travelers are harmed by such drunken people or should even lose their lives. We also reminded him how much the chiefs have forgotten about their responsibility insofar as they admit godless white people, who unceasingly slander God's holy name. These people should be feared and kept at a distance by the people; they have so much contact with the Indians, and through the introduction of strong drink, they almost always keep them drunk. He certainly agreed that we were right and promised to speak about this matter at the next Council.

The Young Wolf

[March 1811] *On the 15th* our friend The Young Wolf,[115] who ate with us at noon yesterday and went from here to Coosawattee, came up to our fence on his way back and asked to speak with his relative, our Alice Shorey. When she went to him, he told her to tell us that he had returned to see us as he promised yesterday. However, he did not want to come to us in the house because he had drunk a lot of whiskey and we, his friends, did not like whiskey. It really was not good to drink whiskey. He would rather come to visit us another time. We were his good friends, whom he did not want to offend since we were good people, and so on. It is a shame that this otherwise really reasonable, well-behaved, and diligent Indian, who is very honored by both brown and white people, sometimes gives in to drinking.

[October 5, 1812] . . . The Young Wolf had us told through our children, who met him in our neighborhood, that he has now completely given up whiskey drinking and wants to bring his daughter,[116] about whom he has so often talked with us, to our school in Dawnee's place.

He believes he had a vision. At least a voice sternly warned him and told him that whiskey would kill him if he did not give it up soon. Since that time, he does not drink a drop.

Sour Mush

[December 1815] *On the 28th* in a thunderstorm, Sour Mush and Watie[117] arrived here. The former was very loud and spoke English, because he was very drunk.[118]

Watie drew him to himself in a brotherly way and led him into another house to quiet him a little bit. When both of them came in the evening to eat, Sour Mush was quieter, and he conducted himself in a reasonable way. At last, he noticed that our house was decorated with green little shrubs and paintings, and he said to his companions: "Presently, I am aware how beautiful this house is decorated; before I was too very drunk to observe it. These people are good for the poor Indians when they conduct themselves as dogs; they do not throw them out of the house, as they would do full well to *white people* if they came in such circumstance to them. They even have compassion for us needy Indians." Our Alice said this in English in his presence.

Chuleoa

[January 1818] *On Sunday the 18th* . . . During our evening devotions, a drunken Indian made a lot of noise screaming in our lane and asked to be let in. This man, named Chuleoa, who has indeed been here before, is a respected man and interpreter between the Cherokees and Creeks.

In the afternoon he was already half drunk here with numerous chiefs who wanted overnight lodging for their horses and themselves. Mr. Hicks[119] attempted to make it clear to them that they themselves would be welcome, but unfortunately it would be impossible to provide feed for the horses since we had only planted a small field last year.

This annoyed the otherwise very reasonable man, and he rode away indignantly. Then he returned, and since our service was not yet over, we had our Michael[120] go out to open the gate for him. After the service, we all went out and found him in the yard with Michael, who led him by the hand into the kitchen. We gave him something to eat and then he was very friendly, called us good people, and immediately afterward went on the road to Coosawattee.

However, in our neighborhood, it was very loud since many Indians had come there to drink alcohol. The Cat,[121] an Indian who comes from one of the northern nations on the St. Lawrence and thus is not very respected by the Cherokees, went into the neighborhood just to watch, not to drink, as he said, and he also returned soon. He himself used to be quite given to drinking but now has become a very sober man and currently stays with our children a lot.

Travelers and Notable Visitors

Springplace attracted Cherokee and non-Cherokee visitors, as the mission and its environs were surrounded by a lane leading to the Federal Road.[122] *Some Cherokees and most American visitors to the mission used horses and wagons as their main conveyances, as road systems throughout the Cherokee Nation began to expand the first two decades of the nineteenth century. Traditional means of reaching the mission were waterways connecting nearby creeks to the Conasauga River. The Conasauga River and its extensive tributary system supported heavy canoe travel, and since most Cherokees lived in riverine communities, their historical waterway arteries also provided the means for communication.*[123] *Springplace served as a hospitality site for a host of Cherokees and other Indians as well as American visitors, including government officials and travelers on their way to the Mississippi Territory or trans-Mississippi lands acquired in the 1803 Louisiana Purchase.*

Chiconehla (Nancy Ward)

[July 5, 1807] *On Sunday the 5th*, Mrs. Vann,[124] the overseer's wife, was present for the praying of the Church Litany, and in the afternoon Mother Vann[125] and Mr. Busby[126] were present for the sermon. The two Indians, who were here yesterday, came again and brought fish. When Brother and Sister Gambold went after the sermon to visit our neighbor Mrs. Vann,[127] who was sickly, they met three very old Indian women from Oostanaula at her place.

They were very cordial toward them. One of them, who is almost one hundred years old, has been a widow for fifty years and is a distant relative of Mrs. Vann. She especially distinguished herself and was very talkative and sincere. She told Brother and Sister Gambold that she is very fond of the white people and that they have always treated her well and that Colonel Meigs[128] always stays in her house when he comes to Oostanaula. When Mrs. Vann told her that we came into this country out of love for the Indians, she shook Sister Gambold's hands with the words, "I am also fond of you."

She also asked about Brother and Sister Byhan, whom she had seen some years ago. This old woman, named Chiconehla,[129] is supposed to have been in a war against an enemy nation and was wounded numerous times, as she herself told. Mother Vann and Mrs. Vann agreed with this. The latter added that she was also an unusually sensible person, honored and loved by both brown and white people. Her left arm is decorated with some designs, which she said were fashionable during her youth. When our children sang some verses, the three old women sat with great reverence and with folded hands.

Afterward Mrs. Vann began to explain the meaning of the songs to them as well as the words of their language allowed, and Mother Vann vouched for her. Brother and Sister Gambold felt very touched by this and they wished Mother and Mrs. Vann the Savior's blessings for their efforts. Upon leaving, old Chiconehla promised to visit us the following day. . . .

In the morning *on the 6th*, old Chiconehla came to our place as she had promised and stayed during school. Afterward we had a long conversation with her. The children translated as well as they were able to in their language what we told her about God's love revealed in Christ Jesus. Chiconehla showed by crying that she was able to feel more about this than she could understand. . . .

She let us know that she wanted to be able to understand the English language because her daughter,[130] who went to school with white people, had heard and learned exactly the good words that we had told her, and also sang and prayed to God every day; she finally became ill and died without fear of death. Now, she added, she is surely in heaven! Certainly, we answered, if she turned to God in prayer in her sickbed and commended her soul to His grace. She seemed very happy but repeatedly expressed her regret that she could not understand the English language. "God understands all languages," we replied. "And even if you speak very softly," added the children, "He understands you." "Now, Chiconehla," we finally said, "We want to pray for you. We pray for the Indians all the time that God might make them just as happy and satisfied as He has made us; we ourselves are also bad people, and without His help, we cannot think or do anything good. We want to ask Him that He would protect you from all evil as He does us and He would let you feel how much he loves you!

And, since you are already very old and may not have too much longer to live, we ask you to say to Him daily, "My Creator and my Friend, You in heaven! Let me feel Your love and increase my love to You! Make good what I have made evil, and so on. And when you depart from this world, just sigh, 'My Friend in heaven! You, Who created me! I would like to be with You in heaven! Take me to You, only because You are so good!'"

Oh, how moved she was! She squeezed our hands tenderly and promised to do so. We asked her whether she knew of other Indians who would like to hear such words, and she answered that only a few old people were to be found at the present time who would like to hear them.[131] Earlier there would have been more of them.

She wished very much to be allowed to bring a grandson to our school. We directed her to Mr. Vann with this concern. In the meantime we showed her our willingness to take him for instruction if she could arrange lodging for him at Mr. Vann's. She then cordially departed and promised to visit us again after a while. What a shame it is that the Cherokee language has no words for the things that are not part of the daily doings and dealings of the Indians! And there are not even enough of the latter. However, the Indians themselves know how to manage well with them.

John Norton

[September 1809] Early in the day *on Sunday the 3rd*, we received a very pleasant visit from four Mohawks, three of whom are half-Indians and can speak English. One of them, Mr. John Norton,[132] whose father was a Cherokee, was the reason for this visit. His father was lured away by the English during the Indian war[133] and instructed in English as well as other useful sciences by an officer who became fond of him. He then went to Scotland, where he married, and then as a British officer in the American Revolutionary War, he came to America again where the above-mentioned, his son, was born.

He took him to England upon his return, where he was given an excellent education. After his father's death, when he was about sixteen years old, the desire rose in John Norton's heart to see his father's people, the Cherokees, and to try to be useful to them. The war[134] with this nation was continuing at that time, and he saw that that he would not be able to achieve his goal then, so he went to the Mohawks, who soon became fond of him and adopted him into their nation. Soon afterward he learned their language, was used by them as an interpreter, and was useful to their nation in many things. Finally he was sent by them on certain business to England, whence he returned three years ago.

It was still his intention to visit his father's nation, and according to the custom of the northern Indians, to cover the corpse of his father with wampum,[135] which he had brought along for this purpose. He was planning to deliver it at the Council, which is supposed to be held in the middle of this month.

This custom is supposed to be of ancient origin if the nation has lost a man in the above manner. In war it counts if a prisoner is brought in his place. He also had brought along more wampum to serve as a word to the wise, whereby he hoped that Mr. Charles Hicks would serve as his interpreter. Mr. Norton seemed to be a very reasonable and well-meaning man; he also had made the very pleasant acquaintance of Brother Latrobe,[136] as well as many Protestant ministers in England. Through him he had received some insights important for him in matters of the Brethren and their teachings. In Fairfield[137] he made the acquaintance of the venerable, now-deceased Brother David Zeisberger[138] and received a good impression of the Indian congregations there.

What makes this man particularly worthy to us is that he believes in the Savior, loves Him with all his heart, and publicly acknowledges that life, salvation, and blessedness are only to be found in His service. He has done much among the Mohawks and turned them away from heathen superstitions so that they now live morally, work diligently, and decided some years ago to abstain from strong drink. To the present time, they have remained faithful to this decision.

The oldest man in his company, a full Mohawk, also seems to be a very dear, upstanding man. He checked out everything he saw here that has to do with stone masonry or carpentry and also asked for some different varieties of garden seeds. His son, a half-Indian, can read English so we handed him one of our little hymnals during the *Singstunde*. After this, he as well as Mr. Norton, sang along very reverently. During the sermon, which Brother Gambold held about Psalm 103:1–4, Mrs. Vann and seven Negroes also attended; our Indian guests were very attentive listeners, too. Norton and the old Mohawk spent the night with us, and in the evening, we had some pleasant conversation with the former.

[October 1809] *On the 16th* we had many visits from friends in the nation, among others Mr. Charles Hicks, who brought us a very friendly greeting from Mr. John Norton. He informed us that he would like to see us and speak with us again before he leaves this area. However, because of the impending winter, he could not postpone his long-planned trip since he would really like to be in his homeland in the Mohawk country before the extreme cold begins. Mr. Hicks also told us that since Mr. Norton had not found an interpreter for the Council in Willstown, his address to the Six Nations was handed over, so that it might be used on occasion by this nation. He would like to have delivered it to his father's nation, the Cherokees; it was being published in London as well as the Gospel of John, which Mr. Norton had translated into the Mohawk language. He added that the true prosperity of the Cherokee Nation lay very close to Mr. Norton's heart, and it was his intention to visit it again.

John McDonald

[October 1809] Early in the day *on the 23rd*, Mr. McDonald also left us. We had some pleasant conversations with this well-informed man. Because he is the only white man in the nation who thoroughly understands and speaks the Cherokee language in the nation and was also raised as a Christian, we put down some words concerning matters of salvation with the request that he translate them. However, he gave us a satisfying explanation that neither he nor anyone else was in a position to do this. Yet he showed his willingness to serve us if it were only within his power. "For things, which do not come up in the trade and commerce[139] of the Cherokee," he said, "they do not have any names, and it is completely impossible to give an idea to things they do not see with their eyes. Yes, generally the language is unbelievably defective." He then gave us various examples of this.[140]

Uniluchfty

[May 1811] *On the 21st* old Uniluchfty visited us accompanied by The Trunk.[141] He said among other things, "I will most likely die as you. I like to hear your words and believe *everything* that you say. You are disposed toward us as *Indians* not as *white people*. We hope that you remain living with us and do not return to your country," and so on. We were sorry that we could not talk with him as he wished, because of the lack of an able interpreter. Meanwhile we had him told a couple of words for his heart through little Nancy, The Ridge's daughter.

Sam Houston

On the 27th [August 1812] a young, very well dressed man from Tennessee came here. His name is Samuel Houston[142] and he brought a letter of recommendation from Mr. Matthew Wallace, in which his request to be allowed to stay with us for some time to profit in some school knowledge was supported. His whole behavior was very charming, and in further conversation we learned that his salvation lies close to his heart and that he would most like to live hidden and away from the noise of the world. When we explained that we were only here for the Indians and could not take any white people for instruction, he decided to travel on to Georgia to see if there was something for him there. Brother Gambold recommended him in a letter to Dr. Brown in Athens, and because the wagon in which he had come here had not stayed here, early *on the 28th* we had our Dick take him to it on horse.

Correa de Serra and Francis Gilmer

[October 8, 1815] . . . Two botanists, who were recommended to Colonel Meigs by the president of the United States, paid us a short visit and ate here at noon. The one, Mr. de Serra,[143] a venerable man, a native of Portugal, also lived in France, but is at this time a resident of Philadelphia. He did not appear to be unacquainted with the missions of the Brethren; he had been also in Gnadenhütten by the Muskingum. The other one, Mr. Gilmer,[144] is a Virginian.

President James Monroe

[May 25, 1819] After . . . it was already very late, a young Mr. James Monroe came riding into our lane with the overseer Birdwell.

When we came to them, the former greeted us cordially and informed us that the president[145] of the United States had just arrived at Joseph Vann's and because there were many in his company, he wanted to trouble us for a night's lodging. He had sent him, since he belongs to his family, to let us know that he was in the neighborhood. He would like to see and speak with Brother Gambold, but he had to travel on tomorrow very early. The overseer asked for some candles for the company, and we gladly served him with this.

On the 26th Brother Gambold got up very early to pay his respects to the president, but had much trouble getting through the bottom, which was flooded by heavy rains. He found him just getting ready to climb into the coach. He expressed our happiness that he honored the Cherokee country with a visit and at the same time our sorrow that time and business did not allow him to see our small institute. The president replied very cordially that he would like to have done this and asked that we excuse him for this. Upon leaving he wished Brother Gambold happiness and blessings. He then left on the road to Brainerd.[146]

Earthquakes

In 1811–12 the Cherokee Nation experienced a series of earthquakes whose epicenter was the New Madrid fault located near present-day New Madrid, Missouri. Had there been a Richter scale, the largest of the earthquakes would have measured 8.0. The tremors fanned out from New Madrid as far as the eastern seaboard and lasted for four months—well into April 1812. Ethnologist James Mooney's informant, Cherokee John Watts, told him that the earthquakes spurred a nationalistic revival movement among the Cherokees.[147]

[December 1811] Early in the third hour *on the 16th*, two shocks from an earthquake[148] were felt. The houses shook and everything in them moved. The chickens fell to the ground from their resting places and caused a frightful crying. At eight o'clock another smaller shock was felt.

On the 17th Chief Bead Eye, his brother The Trunk, and two other Indians came to get information from us about the earthquake. They all seemed very upset and said that the earth is already very old, would it soon fall apart? We explained to them what causes earthquakes, with the comment that the all-powerful God who made the earth and everything on it and until now had maintained it, also had the power and force to punish humans in various ways who live in sin, and that He often had used such earthquakes for just such a purpose.

The residents of this country had reason to thank Him that He was so merciful to them this time and should see it as a warning to stop serving sin and to obey His voice. It was certain that God had determined a day in which He would judge all humans and each one would be rewarded according to his works. Then the earth would be consumed by fire, and so on.

They hung their heads and seemed to be deep in thought. During a heavy rain in the evening, we had the joy of seeing our former pupil Tommy arrive here with his father, our friend Chuleoa and his wife. They were also deeply concerned about and horrified by the earthquake. Chuleoa brought us a letter from Mr. Charles Hicks, in which among other things he reported the following: "I cannot describe the great consternation which we felt last night.

"Our living quarters were moving so much that they seemed close to falling down. Just before this a loud noise was heard from the north-northwest and some people saw a flash of light from right where the noise in the air had begun. This morning, between seven and eight o'clock, we felt two shocks again, but not as strong as the earlier ones and without the slightest noise. Our house, however, shook a lot and the roof was moved. All the trees were also moving without the slightest wind.

"Oh!" Mr. Hicks added, "may we honor [our] merciful God for His protection from day to day and call to Him for help in improving our lives in the future." Mr. Hicks had directed this company, as with the above-mentioned, to us for more exact instruction in the matter. We spoke with them in a similar manner as with the former ones, and our Tommy translated our words with the greatest seriousness.

Our Peggy, who was at neighboring Indians today on business, could not describe in what consternation she found the poor people everywhere. Some of them attributed the event to conjurors and some of them to a great snake who must have crawled under their house, and some of them to the weakness of the earth which, because of its age, would soon fall in. Our Sister took advantage of this opportunity to extol to them the love and the seriousness of God and to advise them to take the salvation of their souls seriously.

[February 1812] Toward evening *on the 3rd*, a small earth tremor was felt.

On the 6th an Indian came to us for information about the frequent earthquakes, and toward evening another Indian, a chief named Daw-gunzi, came for the same purpose. Both of them looked very serious.

We spoke with them in the usual way and they seemed to approve of our words. Dawgunzi said that the chiefs had said some time ago in Council that we were their friends and that they had children of the nation here to be raised by us. Therefore, we should be allowed to make our fields as large as we wanted to.

In the morning *on the 7th* at about 3:30 there was an earthquake and another at 10:30 at night. Everything in the houses was in motion and the roofs creaked loudly. It rained the entire day.

Early in the day Uniluchfty, The Trunk, and two other Indians came and stayed here until evening. Dismay about the frequent earthquakes had also driven them here. They asked us quite urgently to tell them a lot about God. . . . Today we heard from travelers that in Taloney, an Indian town thirty miles from here on the road to Georgia, thirteen sinkholes were caused by the earthquake. The largest of these was twenty feet deep, one hundred twenty feet in circumference, and is supposed to be full of greenish water.

On the 11th The Ridge visited us and inquired thoroughly about the earthquakes. He also said that he had discussed the matter with Mr. Charles Hicks, who told him that God made this happen.[149] Now he would really like to know if the end of the world were not near. We answered him as we had answered the others' similar questions before that no human knows this. It is, however, fitting for us to be prepared always and ready to stand there, and we added what our dear Savior said to His disciples about the matter. The Ridge said, "It is true, we are very bad! May God make us better!" This gave us an opportunity to tell him the whole story of humanity's fall as well and the temporal and eternal unhappiness resulting from this, as well as the great miracle through which the Son of God redeemed us. When we spoke of the sufferings of our Savior, he cried out, "They treated Him *too* horribly!"

[February 17, 1812] . . . In addition, two Indians came who kept us busy a long time. We were very glad that our Peggy was at our place. Through her we were able to speak with them. One of them, The Shoeboot,[150] expressed his concern about the unusual earthquakes here in this country and said with a very meaningful expression, "Many Indians believe that white people are responsible for this because they already possess so much of the Indian land and want even more. God is angry about this and wants to scare them through earthquakes to put an end to this. *All* the Indians believe very much that *God* allowed the earthquakes to happen." . . .

Then the other, named Big Bear, said, "I want to tell you something because I would really like to know what you think about it. Soon after the first time the earth shook so, an Indian sat in his house deep in thought and his children lay sick in front of the fire. A tall *man* clothed completely in tree leaves with a wreath of the same foliage on his head walked in. He carried a small child on his arm and a [*sic*] held an older one by the hand and said that the little child in his arms was God.

"I cannot tell you now if God will soon destroy the earth or not. God is, however, not satisfied that the Indians have sold so much land to the white people. Tugalo,[151] which the white people now have, is the *first* place that God created. He put the *first* fire in a *hill* there, because *all* fire comes from God. Now the white people have built a house on that hill. They should leave this place. Grass should grow on this place and then there will be *peace*. The Indians also no longer thank God before they enjoy the first fruits of the land. They no longer perform the dances in His honor that are traditional in the nation before they eat the first pumpkins, and so on.

"The messenger further told the Indian, 'You are sad because you believe your children are ill; they are really *not* ill, but have just gotten a little dust inside of them.' Then he gave him a couple of pieces of bark from a certain tree,[152] which he named for him. He told him to cook it and give his children the drink, and they would become well from it on the spot. Then he named other means of curing illnesses and finally said he wanted to carry *God* into his house again."[153]

During this cock-and-bull story, the Indian looked as grave as if he were really speaking God's Word and will. We told him that we neither understand such dreams nor get into conversations about them. We hold fast to *God's Word* from which His will is clear to us.

[March 1812] Early in the day *on Sunday the 1st*, an old Indian woman named Laughing Molly came to us in great distress. She asked quite urgently if we would tell her whether the rumor of the Indians has a basis. In three months' time, would the moon become dark again, then would hail stones as big as "hominy blocks" fall, would all the cattle die, and would the earth soon afterward be destroyed?[154] A conjuror said that until then there would be peace. How it would continue he did not know. Now she was, indeed, already old and would presumably not live a lot longer. Still, she did not wish to spend her remaining days in constant fear. Through Peggy we gave her comfort and said that the darkening of the moon is a completely natural event and occurs annually. It also does not cause the earth any harm and also that the Indian rumors are pure lies.

[March 6, 1812] Because another light shock from an earthquake was felt last night, Mother Vann spoke with us once again about this occurrence. Finally we guided the discussion to the main point, that is, God calls to humans to turn to Him. At the same time, we also explained to her the bliss of those who do not ignore such a call. She told us new lies were being spread through the nation. God revealed to an Indian that a great darkness would arise and was supposed to last three days. During this all the white people and also those Indians, who had clothing or household items in the style of the white people, would be carried away along with their livestock. Because of this, they should put aside everything that was similar to the white people and what they had learned from them, so that God would not mistake them in the darkness and carry them away with them. Whoever does not believe this will immediately die along with all of his livestock. This had already happened to an Indian.

Mother Vann added that many had already gotten rid of their household items and clothing. However, she had offered to buy various things from them, just to show them that she did not pay any attention to the lies.

[April 30, 1812] . . . Colonel Meigs had asked Brother Gambold to make this journey to the Council to calm the spirits of the Indians as much as possible. They have been very frightened by the often-mentioned lying prophets. To their joy, however, they found that those present, and especially the chiefs, were seldom persuaded by these things. Instead of spending a lot of time with these things, they undertook practical considerations and agreed upon some necessary arrangements. All the Indians, and especially the older chiefs, were very friendly to Brother Gambold.[155]

When old Chief Sour Mush[156] had once spoken with much affect[157] in the Council, he had Brother Gambold told through an interpreter that he was not angry at all with the white people, but with the misbehavior of his own people's behavior and recklessness.

Among other things in his talk, he told those present, "Recently the earth has sometimes moved a little. This brought you great fear, and you were afraid that you would sink into it, but when you go among the white people to break into their stalls and steal horses, you are not afraid. There is much greater danger, because if they catch you in such a deed, they would certainly shoot you down, and then you, indeed, would have to be lowered into the earth."[158]

Creek War of 1813–14

Indian agent to the Cherokees Colonel Meigs influenced the Cherokees to take up arms against the Red Stick Creeks, and in 1814 approximately six hundred Cherokees, ultimately, aided General Andrew Jackson and the Lower Town Creeks in defeating the Red Sticks at the 1814 Battle of Horseshoe Bend on the Tallapoosa River just east of Emuckfau Creek.[159] *When General Thomas Pinckney ordered the Tennessee volunteer troops to return home without delay, they marched northward from Fort Jackson, crossed the Tennessee River, and heard Jackson bid them farewell in a stirring address in Fayetteville, Tennessee. When the Cherokees returned home, they found their country had been ravaged and despoiled by American troops. The Tennessee militia, disorderly and irresponsible, had stolen horses, killed hogs and cattle, destroyed corncribs and fences, and taken corn and maple sugar, even clothing, from the Indian residents. Indeed, the Cherokees found their homes and families had suffered more at the hands of their white allies than from their enemies, the Red Stick Creeks.*[160]

[July 1813] Very late *on the 12th* in the evening, when the children were already sleeping, The Tyger, our Dawzizi's father, arrived here. We woke his son. Through him, he had us told that he was on the way to the war against the rebellious Creeks[161] and that four hundred men would be marching there under the leadership of the well-known warrior, formerly called Shoeboot, now Crowing Cock. He spoke a lot already about towns burning[162] and so on.

Because the angry Creeks were very dangerous people, he seemed to be somewhat doubtful whether he will ever return to us or he might see his burial there! We had him told that we hoped and wished to see him return soon, well kept and victorious, and eat at our table. He left early *on the 13th* for Coosawattee, where he learned that different orders had arrived. The Cherokees' help was not yet required but should be discussed at a Council.

[August 1813] *On Sunday the 8th* we spent the day in a very pleasant and blessed way with our dear Brother Charles Renatus. . . . He asked us to commend him to all his dear Brethren and Sisters anew in prayer, when we have the opportunity. The critical affairs with our neighbors, the rebellious Creeks, are causing him a great deal of trouble and work from which he would rather be spared. We asked him to be active a little longer for the good of his nation and to rely on the Lord's help. His wish and prayer is for peace, and he untiringly advises his countrymen for this.

[August 1813] Early in the day *on the 17th*,[163] Brother Hicks visited us and brought us the good news that the Council decided unanimously to deny the request to this nation to go to war against the hostile Creeks.

[September 1813] *On the 15th* Nathan Hicks brought us a letter from his father, in which he informs us that the Cherokees are now being requested by the government of the country to move out against the enemy Creeks with the troops of the United States. He had just received an explicit letter from the head chief, Pathkiller,[164] with the news that despite the decision they reached at the last Council not to get involved with this war, the chiefs have now decided to concede to the government's desire. Because of this, he, Brother Hicks, would travel immediately to Colonel Meigs.

[September 24, 1813] . . . He [The Ridge] told us that he was also preparing to go to the war. When we told him that we would diligently remember him and would really be happy one day to see him again in good shape, he replied, "I feel comforted because I believe that my life is in no danger unless the one up high, who has determined the hour of all humans, has decided this about me."

[October 1813] *On the 5th* we sent Dawzizi and Jesse Hicks to the mill again and gave them a letter to our Brother Hicks. In the afternoon his son Elijah arrived here and brought us a letter from his father. He informs us in it that has decided to participate in the campaign against the Creeks, according to the agent's desire, as well as that of the honorable head chiefs. He wants to visit here next Sunday to attend our services one more time and to say farewell to his Brethren and Sisters.[165]

[October 1813] *On the 15th* we learned that The Pathkiller, who lives on the border with Creeks[166] and had encountered several hundred of the hostile party, had sent a fast messenger to Charles Hicks with the news that he was in danger of being surrounded by the enemy party. Because of this, he had a quick messenger recall the Indians, who had traveled to the garrison, to be ready in three days to hurry and aid their old chief. Brother Hicks[167] himself had set out immediately with his neighbors.[168] . . .

On the 16th old Chief Sour Mush, accompanied by his relative, our former pupil George Vann, visited us. The old man was so happy and pleased that he strongly shook Brother Gambold's arm up to his shoulder. He told us that he had been asked by the Vann family to move to the Vann's estate and that he was happy to come to our neighborhood.

We replied that we would also be happy to have him close to us as our friend. "However, now," he said, "First I will go to the war; my sons[169] are also going along." Here he began to cry so loudly that we felt heartfelt sympathy for him. He was also a little drunk. Then he said with a fixed expression, "If I die, it does not mean much, because I am old and worn out. However, if one of my sons is slain, I will revenge his loss through the death of many enemies." He then went into the neighborhood with his companions but returned with them *on Sunday the 17th* to our place for breakfast.

On the 18th our John Ridge's mother[170] returned with another half-Indian from the garrison. She had become very ill on the way, so we prepared her a place to lie down so we could care for her in the best way. Both of them were in great fear of the Creeks and jumped at every noise they heard. Even so, the sick woman slept peacefully for several hours and seemed to be somewhat better on the following day, *on the 19th*. She also ate some chicken soup. She would like to have stayed here until she had recovered more or at least until her husband returned from the garrison, but on account of her children whom she had left at home, the fear of the Creeks left her no peace.

[November 1813] *On the 13th* . . . we had to dedicate our time to two militia companies, each with one hundred men.

They were from east Tennessee and were taking thirty-three wagons to the army in Creek country. They camped on the road below our lane. To our amazement all these people behaved so quietly and in so orderly a manner that we would hardly have known that two hundred soldiers were close to us except that many stopped in briefly and let us know.[171] Some of the officers and also drivers ate with us in the evening. . . .

[December 1813]: *On the 2nd* we heard that a Negro went to Harlan's[172] mill to grind for our neighbors. We ventured to send our John and Dawzizi there, and in the evening, they returned with flour. Jenny Fields[173] also returned from there. She told us unpleasant stories of some of the Tennessee wagoners' wild and indecent behavior, on their return from the army, toward the Indians, mostly women and children whose husbands and fathers were away in the Creek Nation in the service of the United States. She herself was treated very condescendingly, and our former pupil Dick, whose father was also with the army, had three pigs killed before his eyes. A considerable quantity of corn was taken; they threatened him with the most horrible curse words and said that now revenge had been taken on the Creeks and soon the destruction of the Cherokees would be carried out. We were deeply pained, and we commended the matter to Him who judges so rightly and knows how to save the innocent from the hands of the wicked.

[January 1814] *On the 11th* the old Sour Mush, his son, and two other Indians, who had gone with him to the garrison, arrived here very happily in the company of Chief Bark,[174] his wife, and John Beamer.[175] The Sour Mush fetched Sister Gambold, whom he calls his *grandmother*, out of the kitchen and showed her the number of guests he had brought with his fingers. With a thousand joys, we then served these dear guests. When they let us know that they were prepared to go to the war once again, they were once more assured of our remembrance and prayer that our good God might bring them safely to us again.

[March 12, 1814] . . . Numerous Indians visited us today, among others one of Dick's grandmothers with some of her children and grandchildren. The old woman cried unceasingly, because she had learned that one of her sons, who had returned from the war against the Creeks safe and sound and whom she was now on the way to visit, had drowned in the Hiwassee after he had drunk too much whiskey.

[March 1814] *On the 17th* our former bad pupil Moses's[176] stepfather, named Dick Justice,[177] had truly frightened our children. They hurried to us very horrified with the news that this one had taken flight with his family because the Creek Indians were carrying out terrible murders in Hightower. We tried to calm them with the explanation that this, like similar evil rumors which echo from time to time, are most likely just *blind* noise; it turned out to be this way.

[March 25, 1814] Today a rumor came that two enemy Creeks had been seen in Hightower, and measures were taken at a talk there to go after them. . . .

[March 1815] We began Good Friday *on the 24th* also in the most blessed way. . . . In the garden Peggy, with tears in her eyes, said to [Buck], "Oh, my child, we must *never* forget—what the Savior has done for us! . . . We are not worthy, we ungrateful ones: I fear God will punish us on account of our ungratefulness in the way He did the Creeks." . . . Buck cried loudly.

2. Continuity of Traditional Cherokee Cultural Traits

Anna Rosina Gambold recorded matters pertaining to the Cherokees' concept of land, Cherokee body ornaments, food preparation and consumption, conjuring, Cherokee law and punishment, and matriarchal and marriage traditions. Further, she recorded stories the missionaries had heard about rainmaking and about the origins of the Cherokee people, and she conversed with curious Cherokees about Christian images and fixtures. Her very disapproval of Cherokee spirituality piqued her own curiosity enough to record what she heard and saw inside the familiarity of the mission.[1]

Cherokees' Concept of Land and Land Values

However Indians had conceived of land and their own sense of its value, land-hungry settlers aided by elected officials in the newly established republican government demanded their right to move westward. Completely disenfranchised by the United States Constitution, Indians lacked voice, and that fact alone left them to the mercy of trespassing settlers. Moravian missionary Gottlieb Byhan, who recorded the Springplace Diary from January 1, to October 1, 1805, after which the diary's handwriting can be identified as Anna Rosina's, commented on July 3, 1805: "And so one piece of land goes after the other until they have driven them completely out." For example, John Sevier, Tennessee's territorial governor and first elected state governor in 1796, showered his sympathies on invading frontiersmen, whose population exceeded that of United States troops.[2] *Those many emigrants from the Atlantic states preferred going into country belonging to Cherokees. To stabilize white settlement, French traveler F. A. Micheaux noted that people in this part of the country took every measure to avoid any confusion over the rights to property; papers testifying to land titles held the most value.*[3] *Additionally, states willingly granted identifiable parcels of lands to speculators and opportunists before Indians had the chance to negotiate other terms.*[4]

Furthermore land to most Cherokees was not a commodity as it was to white Americans. According to anthropologist Raymond Fogelson, prior to contact, "land to Native peoples could not be exclusively possessed, expropriated, or alienated."[5] *Europeans arrived with the sense of motherland and fatherland, and these terms connoted ownership—and the notion to buy and sell. With their linear orientation, Europeans drew lines and fences around property and allocated property holdings in terms of those lines.*[6]

Gradually, Cherokees began to view land in legal ways. They did not embrace privatization, however, but they began to solidify their identity around holding land in common. Similarly, scholar of Indian studies Nancy Shoemaker has argued that Indians did view land as a "collective territorial sovereignty."[7] *Perhaps artificially, Indians turned to that idea to protect ancestral domains. By 1801 Cherokees had separated out who had "rights to land." Most notably, Cherokees identified the white man in terms of the Cherokee concept of white man's "rights." A white man was a yunek,*[8] *in the sense that a yunek had no "rights to the land." They gave persons of German descent a different connotation. To Cherokees a German was not the same as white man because a German was a "Dutchee"; however, a Dutchee also had no "rights" to the land. So by the early 1800s Cherokees had created their view toward "rights to the land" while striving to maintain their holdings in the Southeast.*[9] *To outsiders, land's worth as a commodity that could be sold and transferred between owners remained the centerpiece of controversy. Consequently, land, both its intrinsic and extrinsic qualities, remained the single most contentious issue in Indian country.*

Beginning with land, this first section of this chapter pertains to Cherokee intrinsic ties to land: rights to land, Cherokee and missionary stances on intruders, Cherokee voices in Council meetings, Moravian attitude toward the United States government, and the Cherokee celebration of lighting new fires as a result of the Treaty of 1819.

A Cherokee Chief

[December 27, 1808] A chief showed us a letter, whereby we learned that the chiefs had decided together that white people, who had settled in this country with no purpose that was useful to the nation, would be driven out of it and that they would all be given notice to move away within thirty days. If not, their houses would be burned, and they would be driven out by force. Arranging this work was one purpose of the calling together of the Indians at this time.

The Flea

[March 7, 1808] . . . One of [The Flea's] comments concerning the constant attempts of the white people to get *more* land from the Indians was very strange, and actually, in certain respects, very well grounded. He had the children tell us that some Indians allowed themselves to be taken in by the white people when they claimed that they were seeking their *true* interests, but actually only had *their own* in mind. Such blinded Indians would also allow themselves to be talked into trading their land for a pittance if the chiefs did not guard against this.

He added that it is basically not *our* earth, it is God's[10] earth. He gave it to us to live on it. He makes grass and corn grow. Otherwise we would not have anything on which to live. One day, when we are all dead, God will burn this earth, which He has given us, and also that which He gave the white people, and so on. He said this and the children listened attentively, etc. Soon afterward he departed very cordially, but said that he would be here, perhaps, again in seven nights because he has business at Vann's.

Johnny Gutseyedi's Uncle

[February 1811] Early in the day *on the 28th*, our young Johnny [Gutseyedi]'s uncle came and complained about great hunger. This was strange to us, because we are not used to this from the Indians at all. Even when hunger is really oppressing them, they sit down very relaxed and wait until something is set before them. However, this man seemed to be in a great hurry. After he had eaten, he told our children that he and three other Indians set the house of a white family on fire last night three miles from here on the orders of the Council.[11]

He added in a very cold-blooded way, "The woman and children sat and cried at the scene of the fire the whole night!" Here it should be noted that for years the Indians had already indicated that those whites, who had come into the country without a profession and settled down, should leave with their possessions. If they did not, the Cherokees would deal with them in the reported manner. However, instead of complying, more of them moved in so that we ourselves doubted whether the Indians would keep their word.

Indeed the latter are so reasonable that they help the residents of a house empty it out without stealing anything. However, if they refuse to clear out, the house will probably be burned down over their heads. Soon after the Indians had gone away, our neighbor Mrs. Crawford[12] came to pick up stockings, which we had knitted for her.

She and her sister had also had an unpleasant visit from four Indians yesterday evening during the evening meal. Her husband had traveled to Southwest Point. Through a Negro, who can speak Cherokee, they informed them that they had to leave the country with their families in three days. They had nothing to fear for themselves. If, however, her husband were home, things might not go so well for him. He had made himself very hated by the nation because of his bad behavior and had also brought many wicked white people into the country. Upon leaving the Indians let her know that they would return in three days and see if their orders had been followed.

Immediately Mrs. Crawford set about packing their things and was not planning to stay here one minute past the designated time. There was an unpleasant feeling about the matter. As glad as we are to see and hear that the Indians finally have become active about freeing their country of people who bring them more harm than good, and as happy as we were to receive hope that through this our neighbor's departure the godless existence at Vann's estate might be stopped, we still could not help but feel pity for these our poor white fellow humans.

[October 31, 1821] . . . We regret that so many bad white people live among the Cherokees. They are an annoyance to the heathen since the heathen, indeed, think they must know things better since they have the great book, the Bible, among them.

Dick

[September 1815] *On the 23rd* Dick[13] came here drunk, together with two other young Indians, their faces painted all over. With force they demanded to eat. We made it known to them that we had nothing prepared. Then we pleaded with them to show a little patience until our midday meal was finished. One was so mean that he threatened to kill us: "What"—he shoved us—"you vile Dutch People here in our land! For you do us no good. I have a notion to kill them," etc. Nevertheless Dick tried to say a word. But probably our presence prevented him. Then they went away angrily. However, they did return, and since our meal was about to be prepared, we called them back. We said to them to take a bowl of beans. Because we had no meat, they were angry anew and threw the beans out of the bowl on a bearskin that serves our children as a bed in their quarters. We were glad that they finally went away. We heard in the subsequent days that Dick himself had likewise claimed the honor of throwing our food away.

Voices in Cherokee Councils

Chief Koychezetel or Warrior's Nephew

[February 1811] Early in the day *on Sunday the 10th*, when Brother and Sister Gambold were visiting Peggy, old Chief Koychezetel[14] was very delighted to see them and told them among other things the following: "So that you know what is going on in the world today," he began his story, "I want to tell what recently happened here in the nation. It has been three nights since I was at a talk in Oostanaula.[15] A man and two women came there; they relayed that when they were traveling, they came upon an unoccupied house near a mountain called Rocky Mountain. They went inside to spend the night there. When it had gotten dark, they heard a noise in the air and thought a storm was coming up.

"Then as they went out of the house to see about this, they saw a whole host of Indians arrive on the mountain from the sky. They rode on small black horses and their leader beat a drum and came very close to them. They were very afraid and wanted so to go back into the house, but the leader called to them, 'Do not be afraid; we are your brothers and are sent from God to speak with you. God is dissatisfied that you so indiscriminately lead the white people onto my land. You yourselves see that your game has gone. You plant the white people's corn. Go and buy it back from them and plant Indian corn and pound it according to your ancestors' ways. Make the people go away. The mother of the nation has left you, because all her bones are being broken through the milling. She will return, however, if you get the white people out of the country and return to your former way of life. You yourselves can see that the white people are completely different from us. We are made from red earth, but they are made from white sand. You may always be good neighbors with them, but see to it that you get your old 'beloved Towns'[16] back from them.

'Also your mother is not pleased that you punish each other severely. Yes, you whip until blood flows.[17] Now I have told you what God's will is, and you should tell others. However, if you do not believe my words, then look to the sky.'

"They did this and saw the sky open, and out of it came an indescribably beautiful light in which were four white houses. From such houses, the leader said, you should build in your old 'beloved Towns.' One was built for Captain Blair,[18] a white man in Georgia, who has already done some spiritual service for the Indians and therefore is much loved by many.

"The others should be designated for other white men who could be useful to the nation with writing and so on. You should also inform Colonel Meigs of everything you have now heard. If you now make it known and there is someone who does not believe it, know that things will not go well for him."

Soon afterward Peggy came for the services at our place. She told us that the old chief desired very much to know our thoughts about this story. He himself believed everything stoutly and firmly; he himself had spoken with the people who saw this vision, and at the Council no one spoke against them except for The Ridge.

However, he was treated badly by others because of this. We were now well aware that the Indians at many Council meetings had already thought up ways of getting rid of the many white people who had penetrated their country. They had already made a number of resolutions for this purpose but until now had not carried any of them out, so we could easily figure out to what end this story was made up. We had the good man told that we could not judge this matter because we did not understand such visions. If there was some meaning to the matter, perhaps it was a dream.

[May 1811] *On the 10th* old Chief Koychezetel, or the Warrior's Nephew, visited us with his wife. He said that he had come to bring us a report from the Council, where he is the most well known speaker. "It is true," he said, "the white people must *all* leave the nation. Yet four blacksmiths, some schoolmasters, and such, who build mills for us, will be tolerated, although they will later go to their own country, and no one should put any obstacles in their way.

"We do not view *you* as *white people* at all, but rather as *Indians*. God sent you to teach our people. You are here to *love us*; not to desire our land. You are only here for our sake. You give us food and drink and do good for our children as though they were your own. You may enlarge your fields if you just want to. No one may drive you away, because you will be seen as belonging to us."

Beloved Women

[February 2, 1817] . . . Jim Foster visited here with his wife, and on account of the prevailing movements in the nation, he talked with Brother Hicks in a very serious manner about several Councils that had been held. The Councils will consider whether the nation will exchange its land with white people for other land across the Mississippi because Cherokees are bothered constantly by the adjoining states about their land. Many appeared inclined to remain here. Several old respected women, who were still the successors of the former "beloved women,"[19] had gathered at Hiwassee, and they had similar considerations because they wanted to remain here. We are quiet about these matters, but we prayed ardently to our good Savior for *true* prosperity for these poor heathens.

Charles Hicks

[July 1817] *On the 19th* . . . Brother Hicks arrived here today. He had many an unpleasant experience at the treaty conference about the Indians' land.

[May 1818] *On the 30th* . . . Our Brother Hicks could not be present because he currently has much troubling business[20] with his poor nation.

Margaret Ann (Peggy) Scott Vann Crutchfield

Below is an excerpt from a letter from John Gambold to Jacob Van Vleck, July 17, 1818, followed by a written copy of Peggy Crutchfield's talk before the July 1818 Oostanaula Council. The transcript of the talk, written in Anna Rosina's handwriting, was found next to the letter in the correspondence folder, Moravian Archives, Salem; transcribed by the editor.

[July 17, 1818] Gov. McMinn had already summoned in May the chiefs to the Agency for a Council "to carry in Effect the treaty of last Year, and to make further proposals for the exchange of their whole Country." But since he had gone beyond the borders of his authority and also appeared in the country under protection of armed soldiers and some cannons, the Chiefs refused to have anything to do with him there but informed him that in June they could have Council session in Oostanally [Oostanaula] where he could present his mission if it pleased him. Since he could accomplish anything else at the Agency, he distributed guns, blankets, etc. to the few who had indicated that they wanted to leave. So [as] he came to the Council in Oostenally, [he] stayed a few minutes in our living room, and was quite friendly to us. I can really not say what he presented to the Council and what was resolved in response, because I have not spoken with Brother Hicks. I have found out this much that the representative[s] of about 50 Towns have disclosed themselves quite emphatically again [against] the emigration, so that one may hope that a large part of the Cherokee will continue living here. At the Council, the women of the Nation have made use of an ancient right to make an urgent presentation to the Chiefs and Warriors to take into the consideration of their true welfare of the Nation. Our Sister Crutchfield was a member of the commission appointed for that.

Her presentation: Oos,te,naw,ly, June 30, 1818:

Beloved Children:

We have called a Meeting among ourselves to consult on the different Points now before the Council, relating to our National affairs.

We have heard with painful Feeling that the Bounds of the Land we now possess, are to be drawn into very narrow Limits. The Land was given to us by the Great Spirit above, as our common Right, to raise our Children, thereon, and to make Support for our rising Generation.

We therefore humbly petition our beloved Children, the Headmen and Warriors, to hold out to the last in the Support of our common Rights; as the Cherokee nation have been first Settlers of this Land, we therefore claim the Right of the Soil. We well remember, that our Country was formerly very extensive, but by repeated Sales it has become circumscribed to the very narrow Limits, which we have at Present.

Our Father, the President, advised us to become Farmers, to manufacture our own Clothes, and to have our Children instructed. To this Advice we have attended in every Thing, as far as we were able. Now the Thought of being compelled to remove to the Westside of the Mississippi is dreadful to us, because it appears to us, that we by this Removal shall be brought to a Savage State again; for we have, by the Endeavors of our Father the President become too much enlightened, to throw aside the Privileges of a civilized life.

We therefore unanimously join in one Meeting to hold our Country in Common as hitherto.

Some of our Children have become Christians, we have Missionary Schools among us, we have heard the Gospel in our Nation, we have become civilized and enlightened; and are in Hopes, that in a few Years our Nation will be prepared for Instruction in other Branches of Sciences & Arts, which are both useful and necessary in civilized Society.

There are some white Men among us, who have been raised in our Country from their youth, are connected with us by Marriage and have considerable Families; who are very active in encouraging the Emigration of our Nation. These ought to be our best Friends, but prove our worst enemies. They seem to be only concerned, how to increase their Riches, but do not care what becomes of our Nation, nor even of their own Wives and Children.[21]

[March 18, 1819][22] . . . the mob is to be feared, presumably this fault is characteristic of all republican governments. There are before our eyes the horrible murders of the Indian in the Lancaster Jail. And that of the 92 unarmed believers on the Muskingum [destroyed Gnadenhütten Mission by an American Revolution militia in 1782] there are others of the same kind. The prospective governments of that time abhorred these methods but had no power to do away with such. That's the way it will happen now. Will our government be able to dare to remove the hundreds of white people to whom Gov. McMinn has granted possession of land with out rent or for free? I believe never! Therefore all the government's love for justice, all its good-will over against the Indians is good for nothing, and so according to my limited insight, only one expedient remains to rescue these poor people from complete destruction, namely to make them familiar with our language, with our laws, and that which the most important, with our and their God and Redeemer, so that at some future time they can be incorporated into the United States, whether as nations or as individuals.

[April 1819] *On the 17th* . . . This week the Indians were very busy completely putting out their old fires and having new fires made by chosen people, as a sign of their joy that the greatest part of their land had been secured. During this solemnity there is also a dance of joy, which, however, did not disturb us.[23]

[July 4, 1819] *On Sunday the 4th*, it was the anniversary of the Declaration of Independence of the United States, and in the morning devotion we thanked our good Lord and God for the rich blessings, in inner and outer concerns, which he has poured out on our dear fatherland since that time, and we asked for grateful hearts and growth in His recognition and love. Even more, however, this happened in prayer before the sermon after singing the One Hundredth Psalm, when Brother Gambold *particularly* mentioned the great good deed which has been shown to the poor Cherokee Nation in these years, because our dear Lord has inclined the heart of the President and other leaders of the government of the United States not only to grant them *law* and *justice* and to assure them the greatest part of their land, but that arrangements were made also by these same people to promote the good of the nation.

Cherokee Agricultural Practices

As Elias Cornelius had remarked in 1817, the Cherokee Nation as a whole appeared to him a "dark and gloomy" place.[24] *The perceived path to "civilization" was the advanced stage of cultivation shown at Springplace with its carefully laid out orchards and rows of vegetal products. Some twenty-five years earlier Washington and Knox fostered the path to the "blessings of civilization," but Indian agriculture still appeared "messy" to white America as Indians planted squash, beans, and corn together in the same fields.*[25] *To gentrify their countryside, Indian agents and missionaries played major roles as negotiators for change that meant total abandonment of Indian farming, dressing, spirituality, and language. If United States lawmakers could devise plans to permit Cherokee males to leave the hunt, a "sport" Europeans considered only as an aristocratic class privilege and excessively exuberant for others, then Cherokees would need and use less land.*[26]

If European notions of agricultural pursuits supplanted the Indian concepts, that would leave "extra" lands to be freed up for cessions, to generate capital for improving their remaining acreage, and assure Indian transformation to a nation of small farmers. Cherokees complied by expressing their willingness to increase their agricultural pursuits but they remained perplexed over land losses and settler encroachment: "Why should we alienate more lands to white settlers?" they asked.[27] *Fertile lands passed to white hands left Indians scrambling for "leftovers," which were sometimes uncultivable.*

Anna Rosina carefully noted hunger among the Cherokees, their failure to learn how to plant orderly orchards, picking unripe apples and peaches, and their sometime condition of beggary.

Hunger in the Cherokee Nation

[December 25, 1810] . . . In the evening two hungry Indian boys arrived here, ate with our children, and spent the night.

We later learned that hunger had driven these poor children from their homeland and that they are currently staying at our neighbor Crawford's[28] under the pretense of wanting to learn English. Oh, it hurts us down to the depths of our souls to see so many desperately suffering people this winter and not to be in a position to help them. But the exception is that we do not send any that come to us away without feeding them; our good heavenly Father has sufficiently provided this for us.

Apple Orchards

[June 1815] *On the 28th* Jim Foster[29] came mainly to discuss the great number of apples stolen by the Indians from our orchard. He promised that this action would be halted and went the next day to neighboring Indians whom he suspected as the guilty ones. Rebuking his neighbors to refrain from such behavior, Foster threatened them with sharp language. Consequently, the orchards for the time being were left undisturbed, and we think that his effort was also not fruitless.

[July 5, 1815] . . . An Indian woman asked for apples in exchange for dried meat since they had been expressly forbidden by Jim Foster to steal any further. We said that it was impossible to accede to her this time, because our apples were still small and unripe. She went away annoyed. One cannot describe how the Indians hunger for this fruit. They come from near and far and often demand these under the pretense that sick ones or little children request them, and they will not eat anything else. In the previous months, they had almost emptied a few trees. Now Dawzizi and Jesse sleep during the nights in the orchard.

Indian Tobacco and Corn

[July 14, 1810] Soon after they[30] had left, Tlaneneh's grandfather Zikilla came, and in the afternoon, Suakee came. He asked us a number of questions including, "From where do corn and tobacco have their origin?" This gave us the opportunity for a conversation with him about God the Creator of all things and Friend of humanity, to which he listened very attentively.

Dawnee's Story

[May 30, 1817] . . . Moreover, Robin's[31] mother appeared very confused and embarrassed on account of certain things and demanded to know what we thought about her following narrative:

She told us her son had heard from his grandfather that an Indian in very old, torn-up clothes on a poor horse had come to his grandfather and suggested that the cultivation of grain would soon come to an end while the earth is too *old* to bear much fruit and that fruit is dying and corn will grow only in the sky.

We were so fortunate just to understand her on account of this saga and to encourage her to be true to her duty, to cultivate her land, and to continue to nourish her children with its produce. Furthermore, however, we left it up to God, Who made the earth and alone knows when the time will be to destroy the earth. She went away satisfied.

Indian Planting

[July 1817] *On the 22nd* an Indian asked us to write up an affidavit that he had killed seven Creeks with his own hand in the last war. Since he intended to make a trip into the northerly region, he thought these residents would then accept him cordially and present him gifts on account of this. There is no use to talking people out of this kind of request, and after he gave us much trouble for a long time and we tried to turn both of them away, just to get some peace, they finally made us bend to their will.

During this time, as his note was prepared, his wife, who had brought a large sack on the horse, was quietly busy filling it up with unripe apples and peaches. A section of our apple trees were nearly empty this season. The diligent Indians plant apple trees themselves, for which purpose we are helpful all the time. But some of them do not wait, rather they think it is enough that they are planted, and subsequently they send for the children or the livestock to have them fall to the ground.

On the contrary, most of them do not plant fruit trees because they will not bring *good luck*. They will not live for fruits! Sometimes peach trees, which grow without their assistance, if their dwelling place permits them, become suitable.

[July 1817] *On the 29th* four Indians came early and offered us money for our apples. We said to them that this fruit was not ripe yet. Their craving for it was so intense that we could not refuse them, so we gave them a few apples as a present.

Cherokee Traditional Rituals and Contact with Christianity

Matrilineality

By the second decade of the nineteenth century, even though Cherokees had adopted Anglo-American measures to facilitate them in their execution of internal and external affairs, other aspects of Cherokee life such as matrilineality within the family unit continued to persist. Cherokee society was matrilocal as well as matrilineal. Cherokee men and women lived separate lives. Women did things appropriate to their gender roles while men performed tasks apropos to their roles.[32] *Perhaps missionaries as strangers in the Cherokee Nation intensified the female role in Cherokee family life and even in Council meetings. John Gambold noted, "The family tree rests on them; the father counts for little or nothing and is able to exercise no more authority on the children than what the mother . . . at least tacitly . . . concedes."*

CHARLES HICKS

[March 1, 1815] *On the 1st,* Jesse Hicks finally arrived. He was held up by high waters for a long time at home with his parents. He delighted us with an affectionate note from his dear father, which said, among other things, "I suppose, Brother Crutchfield has also been absent from the Table of our Lord as well as myself last Saturday, because of the high Waters—but God's Will be done! I hope to be permitted & enabled to be present on our Good Friday, etc."[33] To his pleasure we could report to him that Holy Communion had been moved to the next Saturday for him and Brother Crutchfield, who had asked at his departure that Holy Communion be postponed to the coming Saturday.

Our Brother also attested in the mentioned note his displeasure about the heathen treatment by several old women on his sick grandson.[34] They attempted to dispel his fever by magic, by blowing on him, and such things like that.[35] He, as the grandfather, may not prevent this, because only the mother and the grandmother and the relatives from the mother's side have the right to rule over the child. Our Brother turned himself to our dear Lord in prayer in all such cases.

RATTLING GOURD

[December 3, 1813] . . . Otherwise, today we also had a pleasant visit from our friend The Young Wolf,[36] who was suffering from consumption. In his company were also two of his brothers, The Crawler and The Rattling Gourd.[37]

The latter asked us to take in his daughter Darkey,[38] about ten years old, to educate. We agreed to it. "Deal with her," he had us told through

Peggy, "according to your judgment. I give her over to you, and should she complain to me about *one* thing or the other I will never defend her, but rather you."

[February 1814] *On the 21st* we reroofed our smokehouse and the one on the chicken coop that adjoins it. We had a great many Indian visits including The Rattling Gourd, our Darkey's father. He brought us a turkey, a cut of venison, and a sack full of sweet potatoes. He would not accept any payment for these, because, he said, "Darkey eats some of it too." Few Indians would be so thoughtful![39]

[March 1815] *On the 11th* the mother[40] and aunt of our Darkey visited here. They intimated that they had sent the girl here only for the mastery of the English language and now thought she was skillful in this so that her extended presence no longer had purpose. "Yes, for sure," we let them say. But her long stay here may be even for this reason. Since she understood the language, she was of great use to them and their entire family. If she learned to read God's word and instructed them in it and took it to her heart, then in time she could acquaint her parents and relatives in it. Without this, it would be far better for her if she had not learned the English language. Consequently, to our heartache, we found that the Indians whose English is halting faced harm in very dangerous circumstances from corrupt white people in the land. Indeed, they incited them to become sad examples as we have already seen. They appeared to understand our opinion, and they would let the child stay here yet longer. Dawzizi let with them on a visit to his parents.

[April 1815]*On Sunday the 9th* . . . The Rattling Gourd and his little son[41] were present and stayed overnight. We conversed with the father about the true purpose of his daughter's longer stay here; now she is just beginning to read the Word of God and to understand it in class. We let it be known to him that through Darkey it was possible for her to become a translator for her family. He showed his satisfaction.

[October 1815] *On the 16th* The Rattling Gourd came for breakfast. At the desire of her mother and against *his* wish, he took his daughter Darkey home.

[January 1816] *Early on the 24th*, The Rattling Gourd was here. However, we were not aware of it until he had left. Thereupon we sent Dawzizi to Vann's estate and we had him say, among other things, that we could not understand why he, our friend, had not come into our house and eaten with us, as was his custom. The Rattling Gourd smiled and said to Dawzizi: "I am ashamed to let them see me since I have lied to them. I assured them that I did not wish to take my daughter away from them until they had found it necessary for her to go back home. Yet I took her anyway." The poor man! We really understood him. It was not *his* fault, rather the *mother's*, who made their lives painful until he fetched the girl against his will. The girl had just begun to read the Bible.[42]

Body Ornaments

ISKITTIHI

[February 1807] *On the 17th* Iskittihi, well decorated in the *Indian* way with rings in his nose and ears, returned. With him came the Indian boy Jack, who has often been here. One could clearly see that that latter had recently had smallpox from which he had not fully recovered. Thus we were very happy that they did not stay long, as we were a little worried on our children's account.

[June 1808] In the afternoon *on the 22nd*, our runaway pupil Iskittihi came to our place with two other Indians from Rabbit Trap. They offered us a fish; however, it was already spoiled by the intense heat, and in return, they asked us for something to eat. We gladly gave them something. Iskittihi acted very shy. He wears a very conspicuous ring in his nose!

WATERHUNTER

[March 1810] In the evening *on the 21st* we received a visit from our friend The Ridge, in the company of a young Indian named The Waterhunter,[43] who was unknown to us and whom he introduced to us as his friend. The latter acted very strangely at first, but soon became open and conversational. When we wanted to go to our evening meal, he went silently and took off an unusually large silver nose decoration and did not wear it again during his stay with us. Both of the dear guests attended our Bible reading, which Brother Byhan led. During the singing, they sat completely quiet. However, since the reading lasted too long for them, they began to speak loudly and to look around for drinking water.

When the service was over, we told them the meaning of our reading; they regretted having made a disturbance. We satisfied them by letting them know that we did not think badly of them this time since they did not know the purpose of the service at all.

MARGARET ANN SCOTT VANN (PEGGY)

[December 1810] *On the 31st* the weather was very cold and stormy. Our Peggy had gone to Sumach[44] to buy a couple of pigs from an Indian. She paid for them with part of her former heathen jewelry like earrings, silver bracelets, and such things. She was still here for our closing service although she came late.

ROBIN

[June 1817] Early *on the 24th*, many Indians appeared here again, among whom was Robin's mother[45] and a few of his relatives. Robin, who without our prior knowledge had spent the night with his relatives in a camp, came with them and wore a white feather on his head. As we removed this from him, at the same time, it was said to him that such heathen finery did not suit our Children's Festival.[46] He was insulted and refused to come into our house. His mother, on the other hand, justified our actions. Around ten o'clock, they set out on their journey, so afterward we could commence undisturbed the celebration of our Children's Festival.

Cherokee Marriages: Sororal Practices

According to scholar of Cherokee studies Charles Hudson, sororal polygamy was not an infrequent practice. An advantage was that when a Cherokee male did have several wives—sisters, mothers of sisters, and mothers' daughters from previous marriages— the relatives in these close kinships got along very well.[47]

JOHN ROGERS'S WIVES

[August 1806] Today *on the 8th*, Mr. Rogers's[48] two women,[49] namely a mother and her *daughter*! visited the school in the afternoon.

GEORGE PARRIS'S WIVES

[August 16, 1806] In the afternoon one of Mr. Parris's women visited us with her daughter and her sister's; he has two natural sisters as wives.

Both sons, who are our pupils,[50] accompanied them. They stayed with us for several hours and seemed very pleased.

[August 1806] In the afternoon *on the 25th,* Mrs. Vann visited the school with one of Parris's[51] women, the sister of the one who was recently here, and Rachel Parris.[52] The latter will stay with Mrs. Vann until her husband returns.

[August 1806] In the afternoon *on the 26th,* Mr. Parris came with his wife, who had been here yesterday, to visit the school. He explained to his children in a very sensible way and held a very serious talk with them as well as with our George,[53] who is his relative, about the bad behavior we had told him of.

Cherokee Healing

WILL

[July 1814] *On Sunday the 12th* . . . They[54] expressed their gratitude that their Will[55] was recovering. An old Indian doctor had taken him into his care. He is supposed to be very lucky with his cures, which he carries out primarily through herbs. However, before he accepts patients, he performs a test with little white and red corals, according to an old superstitious custom of the Indians. These are thrown into water and if numerous ones swim, it is a good sign. However, if all of them sink to the bottom, the patient is declared incurable.

PLEASANT

[June 1821] *On the 6th* the children had their doctrinal instruction. Today we received half a deer from the Indian June Buck, for which we gave him powder. Today we also sent for Billy Thompson and asked him to come here and bleed our old Negro woman Pleasant because she has been suffering with a sore leg for a long time. He gladly performed this service for us.

Since the rabbits have caused much damage to our sweet potatoes in the field, we had all our boys go into the field early in the morning with their bows and arrows to chase them away.

THE BIG HALFBREED

[October 9, 1813] He [Charles Hicks] also recently had the opportunity to speak with another chief named The Big Halfbreed about the futility of the so-called magic arts of the Indians.[56] Based on the circumstance that it is known that these impostors are not in a position to either to keep themselves healthy or to prolong their life, he demonstrated to him that they are no more in a position to help others. In connection with this, he took the opportunity to show him that humans were not made just for this short life, but that death had come into the world because of sin and that it pierced its way to all humans. However, God, out of love, had also created redemption for us and in His Word had shown humans the way to attain this, and so on. This caused this chief to reflect a great deal.

[March 1816] *On the 23rd* Brother Charles Renatus Hicks himself appeared. We had a blessed conversation with him. Among other things he related that he had a talk a time ago with old chief, named The Big Halfbreed, about the necessity of converting to God that we have *eternal* souls, and we are by nature all *sinners*. After this life we could not live in eternal joy with God if we do not believe that the *Son of God* had died on the Cross for our sins. We attain forgiveness of all our sins through His blood. Whereupon the old chief repeated, he could not grasp this. Perhaps he would learn to understand something about it if one repeated it often enough to him.

Our Brother also pointed out to him the futility of all conjuring, which the Indians also hold in *very* high esteem. He asked him whether he could believe that a conjuror's immersing a man into water[57] could protect him from sickness or could save a man from death when he saw how many people got sick often and also died regardless of these tricks. The Big Halfbreed answered that he considered this fully. Only he still did not understand what our Brother had said to him before and was resolved for the time being to remain with the *ancient beliefs*.

Then we reported to him that shortly before, Polly Blackwood,[58] the daughter of Sally McDonald,[59] who lived at the Brother and Sister Crutchfields', was taken back home at the request of her grandparents, her mother's parents, for a few days, because the conjuror had arrived. Brother Hicks said that such things even happened in his house with his eldest children. However, our Brother told us that he had examined the deeds and it did not take place anymore with his younger children. The conjurors pretended, through magic, to bring about health once again by immersing children into water to heal them.

Cherokee Burial Practices within the Description of a Slave Funeral

[November 9, 1808] In the morning *on the 9th* was the burial, which Brother Gambold led at Mrs. Vann's request. According to Mrs. Vann's own testimony, she would like to have her dear Negro woman[60] be remembered by her in her last days and what she had experienced in her own heart by the sick woman's bedside for the rest of her life. But the overseer[61] had a grave dug for her at Mr. Vann's order in the woods at the place, where the three criminals[62] were executed and buried three years ago. Brother Gambold also gave the burial address there to a small procession of blacks. He quite urgently asked those present to turn today to Jesus Christ, the Savior of all humanity, in order to become free from the rule of sin through His sacrifice and death, to be reconciled with God through His blood, and finally to become heirs to eternal life. Many tears were shed, especially by Mrs. Vann. Our children were also very touched.

This was a completely strange scene for them as well as for young Nathanael Byhan[63] since the latter had never seen a corpse, and none of them had ever seen a burial. The Indians generally give the corpse to a certain man for burial; he buries it in private and then has to distance himself from other people for a number of days and is not allowed to go into any house.[64] His food is given to him in containers, out of which no one is ever allowed to eat again.

. . . The corpse also had a very pleasant look, and we have the faithful hope that the loyal Savior has taken her soul to Himself in grace. This Negro woman was born in Cherokee country, and like the Indians themselves, was raised ignorant of God and godly things until she moved here last summer and sometimes visited our services. She had a very honest disposition on account of her mistress, who loved and protected her to an unusual degree.

Other Cherokee Death Practices

[April 1811] *On the 6th* we heard, to our sorrow, that our good friend Suakee had died after a long illness. Supposedly, his wife[65] neglected him greatly during his illness, according to the manner of the heathen, so that he was not at all recognizable to his friends who visited him, because of the filth on his face. A couple of Negroes from our neighborhood buried him.

[May 1811] Early in the day *on the 11th*, our friend The Gunrod brought Mr. Charles Hicks's son named Jesse, who is about nine years old, to our school. At the same time he delivered us a very friendly letter from Mr. Hicks containing the Declaration of the Council concerning our mission, which we had already received from Colonel Meigs.

Poor old Gunrod had left his family since he noticed that he was no longer pleasant in his house because of his illness and long-lasting continual coughing. On account of it, he is prevented from working as diligently as before. He had gone to his relative Mr. Hicks,[66] where because of his upstanding nature and faithfulness, he is loved and treasured.

[May 1811] Early in the day *on Sunday the 12th*, The Warrior's Nephew[67] and his wife[68] were here again. The poor man is almost blind, and it is feared that from his wife's side, who is not as good-natured as he is, things might happen to him in the end as they did to old Gunrod. We have true compassion for him. He is really our true friend. We do not know how to help his sight, although he asks for advice on every visit.

Peggy brought her relative Gunrod and three of The Trunk's children along to the services, and afterward she explained to them the purpose and meaning of them. During the praying of the Church Litany, five Negroes were present. During the sermon about the gospel text for today, seven Negroes were present.

Cherokee Rainmaking Practices

According to noted scholar of Southeast Indians Charles Hudson, Cherokees, unlike the Creeks, had weather controllers who were priests. These ritual practitioners performed other ceremonies as well.[69]

DROUGHT

[July 1811] *On Sunday the 28th* . . . After a long drought, it rained the whole past week, and today it rained unusually heavily and unceasingly the whole day. Peggy told us that a couple of days ago an Indian woman had been at her place who had told her that the country has a certain famous rainmaker to thank for this rain. Her townspeople had undertaken a journey to him because of the long drought. He was also immediately willing to serve them. First of all, however, he ordered them to hunt a deer and bring it to him. Secondly, they should choose seven men and the same number of women from their town, who should abstain from all food and only eat something in the evening for seven days.

They must also agree to sit together under the open sky during the seven days, and if rain followed, to dance during it. On the seventh day, however, when the rain would be unusually strong and long lasting, they should dance throughout the night. Then the weather would change again and become clear and bright.

Peggy tried in vain to convince the poor person of the futility of such things and to prove to her from God's Word where rain and fruitful times come from. However, she had no ears for this, but remained firm in her opinion, which irritated Peggy silently; she made her sigh to the Savior. As often, she complained to us in tears that her words find so little entry among her countrymen. "Oh," her usual words are, "if they only knew how good I have it with the dear Savior, they would certainly long for them! . . . .

Meanwhile it did not stop raining after the seventh day as the rainmaker had predicted, but continued raining heavily for several days. However, the blinded people do not pay attention to that, and the one, who was surely well paid for his claimed skill, will be well cared for with provisions throughout the winter; he knows how to convince them in all sorts of ways why this or that work can vary.

There are numerous members of this profession here in the country. If they are not lucky enough that rain follows, then they have enough excuses to keep the *unknowing people* well disposed toward them. Either it is blamed on the *unbelief* of one part of the nation—because many of them really do not believe such stories anymore—or on some other cause such as, for example, the Indian are becoming more and more *evil*.

THE BEAD EYE

[July 1813] Early in the day *on Sunday the 25th*, The Bead Eye, who was going around the country announcing a Council in twenty nights, arrived here with a letter from The Big Halfbreed; in it he asks for the so-called magic corals with the offer of good payment. Our Peggy let us know right away that the Indians use such corals not only with people who are sick, but also for *rainmaking* and that The Bead Eye is one of the *Rainmakers*!

There he sat very quietly and seriously and lamented yet his *really young* corn! At this time many such conjurers are busy, and because their efforts have been without the desired results until now, one blames the other. From time to time severe fights arise out of this.

Trade

Trading was part of everyday life. Anna Rosina recorded the dailiness of trading as ordinary mundane occurrences. Sometimes she mentioned trade items in a cursory way, but other times she went into great detail when a family was totally absorbed in trade items.

As John McDonald told Anna Rosina, "For things which do not come up in the trade and commerce of the Cherokee, they do not have any names, and it is completely impossible to give an idea to things they do not see with their eyes. Yes, generally the language is unbelievably defective."

[March 1805] At three o'clock in the morning *on the 6th*, the Indians, a number of whom were relatively drunk, actually came back again. One stayed in the barn but made a horrible racket until he finally fell asleep. The others came again into the schoolhouse, where it was also rather noisy. However, they did leave us in peace. The drinking lasted until noon, when all their brandy had been consumed.

We heard that one of them had given his flint pistol for a quart of brandy. Finally, in the afternoon, they fell asleep and slept until almost evening, when they were somewhat sober. In the evening another old Indian arrived; he had sweet potatoes to trade. We traded with him and gave him some sewing needles for them. He spent the night with us. *On the 7th* our guests went on their way.

In the afternoon *on the 8th*, Cherokee Chief Chuleoa came to our place from Southwest Point. He had brandy to trade. He spent the night with us. Mr. Vann had also bought spirits from him and paid $1.00 for a quart, which is the usual price among the Indians.

[January 26, 1806] . . . Many Indians came today and forced fourteen turkeys on us.

[March 5, 1806] . . . Today we were very fortunate to trade with a couple of Indian women for some earthen containers. For a long time, none has been brought here, and we were almost in trouble because we were very short on them. Four Indian women spent the night.

[April 1806] In the morning *on the 5th* . . . Brother and Sister Gambold visited Vann's old place. An Indian brought us fresh fish, which is very rare here.

[August 5, 1806] . . . At dusk an Indian woman came. She is known to be very needy and wanted to trade baskets for linen to make shirts. We told her that we do not have it for sale. However, since we really wanted a couple of baskets, we offered her some trinkets and gave her food to eat, which really greatly pleased her.

[March 7, 1808] Soon afterward some Indian women came for the last time *for the present*. They are relatives of our Johnny.[70] They have provided us plentifully with meat since the end of January and brought us several more turkeys and cuts of venison. These Indian women and their families live in Oostanaula. Because of hunting,[71] they had stayed for some time on the Conasauga, about five miles from here.

There they erected two huts. The men were very diligent in hunting, and the women were busy with basket-making and such things. We saw these Indians as our providers, sent to us by God, and we thanked our dear heavenly Father for this great help that was given to us through them. On their hunts they also killed *wolves*, which a Cherokee does not do easily, along with foxes and other dangerous animals. Through this they have acquired a great number of furs. They sold the meat, which they brought us, for a very cheap price and did not take much of our time with their trading. Usually they came twice a week and brought so much that we could salt down a lot of venison cuts for use in the summer.

From time to time they also brought us wax, which was of good use to us since we were completely out of tallow for candles. Our children had visited them three times in their camp, and each time they sent them to us laden with meat. Then the next time, when they came themselves, they received payment for this. It happened a number of times that one or the other asked for something for which they had not brought enough meat.

When he was told this, the answer was, "Just keep it. I will bring *more* the next time and only then will I take the payment." A young man, who wanted to go to the garrison with others, desired an old scarf and offered three cuts of venison for it. We told him that the scarf was still good and worth four cuts.

His answer was that he would gladly give us the fourth cut for it; however, he was just about to go to the garrison and wanted to wear the scarf. We took a chance and gave it to him. The following week he brought a nice turkey and asked if we would accept it instead of the cut of venison, which he still owed us, because he could not find any deer. We gladly accepted this and were delighted by his honesty. In short we found in this Indian family an unusually truthful people. When they came today for the last time, we bade farewell very warmly. However, we were happy that they were going home now because the weather will not allow us to store fresh meat anymore.

[April 1808] At noon *on the 2nd*, a well-dressed Indian couple came with a very neat[72] little child and showed themselves to be unusually friendly toward us. They offered us a large paddle, a kind of sieve, and an earthenware bowl for a quart of *scouring soap*, and were very thankful that we *agreed* to this trade.

[April 13, 1809] When we arrived home, we found Brother Joseph Gambold, who had stayed alone to watch the premises, busy with two Indians, who had brought turkeys to trade.

[December 24, 1810] Tlaneneh's mother and uncle also visited us today. They had chickens to trade.

[May 1821] *On the 18th* for the first time in months, we were once again able to trade for a half deer with powder. When the Indians are busy with their fieldwork, little or no hunting is done.

Cherokee Law and Punishment

The inner workings of the Cherokee legal system eluded Anna Rosina. The basis of the Cherokee traditional legal system was the seven clans that dictated Cherokee behavior both in the family and in the broader society.[73] *The female side, not the male, determined kinship. Clans united the Cherokees into one nation, one people. According to legal scholar John Phillip Reid, the clan was the "corporate entity based on kinship."*[74] *Clan governance began to crumble as Anglo-American settlement went unabated. Pressure mounted for the Cherokees to question their clan-based legal system. In 1810 the National Council passed a law that said that any past or future injuries could not be resolved by blood revenge. Thereafter, the killer himself would be accountable to the Nation for the murder, and the clan could no longer demand a life.*[75] *Legally, the Nation, instead of the clan, assumed responsibility for punishing crime.*[76] *However, the concept of clan-based retaliation remained pervasive at least through Anna Rosina's tenure in the Cherokee Nation.*

She did, though, unveil the Cherokee light horse brigade and Cherokees' use of corporal punishment. As young Cherokees who wanted to emulate their ancestral warrior class began to steal horses from settlers and fellow Cherokees, the Cherokee National Council in 1799 established the light horse brigade, the Cherokee police force, to protect Cherokees from robbers, horse thieves, and in general harmful behavior from fellow Cherokees. But Cherokees' sense of law and order also ushered in European ways of dealing with errant behavior: corporal punishment. According to legal scholar and historian Tim A. Garrison, the sanctity that Cherokees gave protecting the individual and community stems from their shared sense of spiritual sovereignty.[77]

Lighthorse Brigade

[November 9, 1807] . . . In the evening there were seven loud shots close to our fence, one right after the other and immediately afterward at Vann's. We all ran into the courtyard but could not see anyone. On the following morning, *on the 10th*, we learned that it had been the Regulators or Lighthorsemen[78] of the nation, who are responsible for keeping order in the country and who had announced their arrival at Mr. Vann's in *this* way.

[December 27, 1808] . . . Another aim was to properly punish the thieves in the nation itself, as many of them as could be found, because this disreputable business is ever increasing. Two thieves were brought in at Vann's already this evening and bound. One of them received one hundred lashes, the other received 130. Afterward the latter was bound with chains around his neck and legs; however, he escaped when his guards had fallen asleep.

On the 28th five thieves were punished. It was strange that those who received the punishment immediately afterward received orders to help with the beating of their brothers in crime.

[February 1809] In the morning *on the 8th*, Joseph Vann went with his father on a journey to go through the country to punish thieves in the company of a number of Indians. The boy cried and did not want to go along; the father, however, forced him to go.

[May 1809] Early in the day *on Sunday the 14th*, ten Indians came from the Lighthorse Brigade; they were very friendly and spoke about their activities, how many thieves they had already punished, among others also an old white man, and so on. Then they requested that Brother Byhan play the organ for them. He did this, and the rest of us sang along. At the beginning they laughed loudly with pleasure. We told them that we *praised God* in this way. Then they became very serious and listened quite reverently.

The James Vann and John Falling Duel

[January 1806] To our sorrow *on the 20th*, we heard that our dear neighbor, Nancy Falling, had been picked up by her husband[79] during the night on Saturday, along with all of her household goods. He had taken her to his place, apparently out of fear for her brother, Mr. Vann, who is not at all happy with her marriage to Falling. Meanwhile she was away from him[80] as he was shortly expected home.

[May 1806] *On the 15th* . . . Mr. Tynor[81] came during the service and sat down with us. Afterward he notified us that Mr. Vann had received and accepted a challenge from his brother-in-law, John Falling,[82] a thoroughly bad man who has threatened his life for a long time.

One cannot describe how we felt when we received this news. . . . Then when everyone had just gotten to sleep, Brother and Sister Gambold were awakened by a hard knocking on their door. To the question, "Who is there," came the answer, "Jemmy Vann's mother." Brother Gambold hurried to let in his old mother. Immediately she collapsed with loud sobbing around the neck of Sister Gambold. Sister Gambold thought

Mrs. Vann's son was dead and said that God our Savior would provide comfort. But she cried, "Jemmy has killed Falling." Then she went on to say that the latter had ridden toward her son—one and a half miles from here—and when Vann glanced at Falling, Falling made a loud cry. When they had gotten as close as possible, they fired at the same time. Falling's charge hit against Vann's *rock wall*, so that the fire hit it and at the same time Vann's charge went through Falling's chest and threw him dead to the ground. His brother, who was with him, sought to get Vann in a treacherous way afterward. He hid himself behind the trees and took aim at him but fortunately the latter escaped.

His old mother fervently asked Brother Gambold to go with her immediately to her son, who might want to see him.... Brother Gambold himself was willing and went with her. He found Mr. Vann quite conscious....

Early on the 16th, he went there again with Brother Byhan in order to visit Mrs. Vann and old Mother Vann and to comfort them in their distress. Mr. Vann had actually set off before daybreak.... Brother Gambold had advised him to stop in at the chiefs on his journey in this area in order to explain thoroughly the entire series of events. He promised to do this, and it is also extremely necessary because Falling's relatives will attempt to twist the matter to his disadvantage and among these there is one chief,[83] who has been his sworn enemy for a long time....

Mrs. Vann sent us a nice piece of goat meat for a meal. Toward noon Sister Gambold went to visit her. His old mother had gone home. She found Mrs. Vann still crying and very upset about her husband because his life was being threatened severely by the relatives of the deceased.[84] ... Toward evening his old mother visited us.... Her poor daughter Nancy is very much in her heart and in ours. She is very distressed about it, and about how she herself should have her[85] fetched from Falling's house. The Negroes and Indians are afraid to go there because they fear for their lives.

Consequences of Vann's Duel with Falling: Clan Retaliations

JOHN ROGERS'S REQUEST FOR A PLACE FOR HIS DAUGHTER

[March 1806] *On the 14th* Mr. Rogers, who lives about forty miles from here, came and asked if we would accept his daughter,[86] a girl of twelve years, into our care. He said that it really concerned him that she, in addition to learning sewing and knitting, should learn reading, writing, and arithmetic. She has already been to several years of school; she could read the New Testament and has also made good progress in arithmetic. Here she has the opportunity to practice *these skills* even more and to learn practical work. What most concerned him was for her to develop her mind and her heart and to learn to live in the way necessary to get along among well-mannered people. She would have to do without all this if she stayed with her mother, who is an Indian.

[March 16, 1806] Afterward Brother Gambold went to Mr. Vann in order to discuss Mr. Rogers's request with him and to get his opinion about the matter. Mr. Vann agreed with us, that if Mr. Rogers stopped in again to ask about taking his daughter, and if we decided to fulfill his wishes, then it would be good for him to introduce the matter to the chiefs at the upcoming talk. If they did not have anything to say against it, then he should try to arrange it so that his child would be accepted in the place of Iskittihi, who ran away, and have her declared as the fourth child in our care.

In our evening conference, we considered the matter thoroughly, and finally laid it before the dear Savior, who gave us a sign through the lot that we should accept the child for *a trial period*.

[March 24, 1806] At the talk [Mr. Rogers] promised to take care of everything that we presented to him. He even offered to let Iskittihi be taught by *his* schoolmaster, if he returned, should he want to go back to school. He had had a school where Mr. Vann's two children, Joseph and Mary, were also taught.

[June 1806] In the morning *on the 30th* . . . Mr. Rogers was very friendly. He gave his opinion several weeks ago concerning his daughter coming here, which is that despite the fact that she is healthy again, he did not want to risk sending her so close to Mr. Vann *for the time being*, whose *friend* he surely is, as the child's mother is Falling's sister.[87] We also heard that the matter concerning Vann and Falling was discussed at the talk and the chiefs had excused the former even though the relatives of the *latter* are still after revenge.

[July 1806] *On the 9th* . . . It was an unusually hot day, but nonetheless we found it necessary to accept Mr. Vann's invitation to eat the midday meal with him. He was very lighthearted and talkative and told us that he could visit us but all kinds of threats from the side of the Falling enemies have reached his ears—even that they would burn his house down over his head. He is not really afraid but it seems necessary to him to sit and not take a chance on leaving his house without an escort for a while. He was also surrounded by loaded weapons.

ARCHIBALD FIELDS

On this occasion we also learned why Archibald Fields was picked up and taken home so suddenly during Vann's absence. His father, who is also Falling's relative,[88] was supposed to be very active in inciting others against Mr. Vann, in order to threaten his life.

DISTANT DEW

[April 1819] *On the 26th* . . . The boy Distant Dew[89] had treated young Squatisele[90] roughly and in his anger almost taken out one of his eyes. This and one side of his face were completely swollen. Thus we found it necessary to let the parents of the injured boy know, since they only live three miles from here. They came here today in Sister Crutchfield's company and acted very reasonably. They asked precisely whether their son had given cause for this. If this were the case, they wanted to punish him as well as the other. They were told that their child had not given cause for this. Then the woman said to her husband, "I will punish Distant Dew. He is from my family," meaning from the same clan,[91] at which she gave him a number of blows as well as a serious talk, and upon leaving she said to us, "If his mother comes to you and says she is offended, then just send her to me!" To our joy Distant Dew seemed very humble.

RATTLING GOURD'S FAMILY

[March 1821] *On the 21st* our pupil Tony, The Rattling Gourd's son, was suddenly fetched home. Later we learned that his older brother who lives in Coosawattee had fatally wounded another Indian while drunk. Thus the parents feared revenge in case he died and brought their children into safety.

[August 1807] *On the 12th* . . . Today we also received the news that the well-known Chief Doublehead, while sitting on a horse in the last several days at a ball play[92] on the Hiwassee, was shot by the Indian The Ridge. Still alive, he was carried by his friends to our friend Mr. Blacke's[93] house, where he was finally killed with a hatchet by another Indian the next morning.[94] Mr. Blacke and his family fled to the other side of the Hiwassee. Doublehead, who had become displeasing to the chiefs in our area some time ago, had caused his death, which had long been threatened,[95] when he engaged in an exchange of words with an Indian at the ball play and hit him on the spot. The Ridge immediately took the opportunity to plot against him. They also went after Doublehead's brother,[96] but he got away safely.

[February 1809] Early in the day *on the 21st*, the horrible news of *Mr. Vann's* murder[97] was brought to us. After he had already gone here and there in the country holding the strictest trials, he had an Indian, who did not give himself up willingly, shot. The miserable man, Mr. Vann, had stopped and gotten really drunk for several days at an inn about thirty-six miles from here; it belongs to Tom Buffington, a half-Indian.

Then he got into a fight with some of his former friends[98] against whom he had long harbored a deep grudge and treated extremely contemptuously; he threatened them with the most horrible intimidations. Toward midnight, when Vann was at the table, which stood across from the open door, a shot was fired from outside and hit him directly in the heart. Immediately this threw him dead on the floor, without anyone being able for sure to report with certainty who had done it.

His young son[99] was sleeping upstairs in the house and he, wrapped up in a blanket, fled with a Negro in the middle of the night to another of his father's plantations on the Chattahoochee,[100] eighteen miles from Buffington's.[101] At once, after the shot, all of his clothes he had with him, like his father's, as well as other valuables including his pocketbook containing a large sum of money in banknotes, were stolen. Thus fell this man, who had for so long been feared by many, but loved by a few, in his forty-first year.

[February 1815] Early *on the 9th* . . . The Ridge arrived here and presented reason for a serious discussion about the fall and redemption of mankind. The Ridge said, "Charley—Brother Hicks—says the same to us; he takes pains with the Indians, yet many despise to hear about Christianity. Charley and Peggy are good people and would like to see all Indians become equally *good.* I myself yearn to hear of such goodness. In my youth I killed a mean Indian and since that time, I have been embarrassed many times to know whether God would punish me for it someday. I decided never to do such a thing again unless the Council commanded me to dispose of a wicked person as was the case with Doublehead."

Cherokee Corporal Punishment

In an 1811 council, Koychezetel or Warrior's Nephew reported to the missionaries a vision some fellow Cherokees experienced. Among other things revealed to the Cherokees, they were told: "Also your mother is not pleased that you punish each other severely. Yes, you whip until blood flows."

[April 1811] *On the 29th* The Ridge arrived here and acted very friendly. However, on the following morning *on the 30th,* his behavior seemed very suspicious to us. He paced back and forth in the yard with one of his very serious expressions and individually spoke with his and his brother's son. The latter cried a lot.

We were in great distress about what this kind of behavior might mean. Finally, The Ridge also called our Johnston,[102] who still lay sleeping in the schoolhouse, and ordered him to tell us that Gutseyedi, who is called John here, treated young Buck, his brother's son, in the worst way, yes *gruesomely,* and tried to lead him to evil things. "Such things," he added, "I would not have expected here! Oh, how the poor young boy's father and mother will cry when they learn of this!" We answered him that we did not know anything about all of this and that we did not tolerate such things here at all.

Unfortunately John Gutseyedi had learned *many bad things* through his two long stays at his relatives' place. This was well known to us. However, to learn of such things was completely a surprise[103] to us and it certainly bothered us as much as him. He answered, "If you do not have anything against it, I will chase the bad young boy from here with a whip, because he does not belong among our children." We said we did not have anything to say against this. Then he had him sought after, because he had hidden himself. After he had given him a couple of good lashes with the whip, he told him to go to *his relatives*. The miserable boy stood there as if turned to stone, and we called to him with tears in our eyes, "Go John, it is your own fault! You did not want to have it any better! . . .

We gave him some bread to take on his way as he lives a good day's journey[104] from here, and then turned away to mourn silently the unhappiness of a boy who had formerly been so promising. . . . The other children with whom The Ridge also spoke seriously were thus shown that not only we, but also well-mannered heathen from their nation, believe in discipline and order.

Cherokee Punishment of Missionaries: Hiring a Conjuror

Since these were volatile periods of sociopolitical turmoil, persons like Dawnee employed conjurors, who attempted to locate the cause of irrational suffering; she thought she could victimize and punish the Gambolds with a "fix."[105] *Perhaps in her own way she also tried to mitigate her own psychological tension. In resorting to hiring a conjuror to right a supposed wrong, Dawnee employed Cherokee spirituality reflecting a well-ordered social system that dictated what the late Cherokee anthropologist Robert Thomas called the "harmony ethic."*[106] *Thomas argues that Cherokees paid scrupulous attention to preserving "harmonious interpersonal relationships by avoiding offensive behavior or promoting the negative side."*[107] *Cherokee scholar Fred Gearing points out that a corollary to the Cherokee "harmony" ideal is that "direct, open conflict is injurious to one's reputation."*[108]

[May 1816] *On the 11th*, at the time the children had already gone to bed, late in the night, Dawnee, mother of our Robin, arrived here for a visit.

Early *on Sunday the 12th*, this mother left with the excuse that she had left something in The Trunk's house in our neighborhood. She merely wanted to take her son there. But we soon discovered that she had brought a conjuror with her and had left him in *the* house in order for him to perform magic[109] on her son. Such things happen from time to time but are kept very secret from us so that we find out about it only accidentally. Moreover, this woman, who is an ignorant heathen, legitimized her actions and conduct toward her son with other intentions, as if she were a rational mother.[110] Her son had complained to her about our bad treatment. Then, as she made her trip back from The Trunk's house, he hid with her until afternoon in the woods, and thereafter stopped in our lane. She did not come near us.[111] At last, the children overheard that Robin had sometimes lied to her and tried to expose to her our bad treatment; with this she became enraged against us. We requested they come to us in order for her to tell Sister Crutchfield[112] of her son's bad behavior.

As this happened she accosted him very sharply in her own language and tried to bring about a confession from him that he had lied to her. He would not do this completely, whereupon she led him into the house and through whipping forced a confession. This was a rare occurrence of an Indian woman against her child.[113]

Traditional Methods of Healing and Punishment

[September 1814] *On the 20th* we received a visit from our Dawzizi[114] who has recovered fairly well. He said the old Indian doctor had *scratched* his whole body and rubbed it with the juice of certain herbs. This operation is performed with a saw-shaped lower jaw of a fish[115] in the waters here; long stripes are pulled through the skin at small distances by it, so that it then looks completely bloody. The Indians put great stock in this; they also use it as a method of punishing their children in order to make them *better*. Our children often carry this out on each other, as they say, to make themselves *nimble*. Dawzizi also said the doctor extracted a little horn of blood from his forehead and back of his head, which provided him with the desired effect against headaches.

Green Corn Ceremony

Southeastern Indians placed great significance on the Green Corn festival, or Busk, as known to the Creeks. The ripening of corn was a dominant feature signaling the beginning of a new year. It made life not only possible but also meaningful. The Green Corn ceremony was a time of peace and forgiveness, communion, and sharing. It was a time to repair relationships, purify the body through emetics, and begin anew. Celebrating the forthcoming bounty of life (i.e., corn) initiated the beginnings of a new spiritual world invoking cosmic order. Smoke arching upward from newly lit fires, the smell of roasting green corn ears, and dancing sustained a sense of spiritual sovereignty and community.[116]

[July 1808] *On the 26th* our Dick's mother and aunt visited us. The mill is not working again, and furthermore most of our old corn was rotten so that our children are very happy to eat fresh Indian corn and also potatoes instead of bread. Thus we offered our dear, apparently very hungry, guests this food as well. They, however, shook their heads and said that they would certainly eat *potatoes* but they did not want to eat corn because they had not been *scratched*. Each year before they begin eating the new corn, this operation is carried out by the headman[117] for the old and young who belong to his family. Using a sharp fish bone, he makes scratches over the chest and back crosswise, on the arms and legs, however, in long stripes, so that they become completely bloody. After this is done, a family dance follows, and then they begin to eat the new corn happily. This is also what happens when they eat the first fresh beans in the year. Indeed, in this case, a good medicine and a day of fasting are supposed to do the same thing with respect to their health. Everyone who belongs to the clans where this custom is practiced has to undergo one of these methods.[118]

[September 1819] *On the 9th* . . . In the meantime The Tyger, who had been at the Green Corn Dance, returned here.

Ball Play

The "mini-warrior" sport, ball play, was a frequent occurrence during the Early Republic. Ball play required players to subject themselves to a specific course of rigorous training and conjuring. The season began around the middle of the summer and lasted until it was too cold "to permit exposure of the naked body." Since players belonged to different settlements, the players' shamans entered into the hotly contested game, too, as they performed their own "special incantation" to invoke defeat, death, or render persons of the enemy camp disabled.[119]

The players usually met on an open field where they stripped except for a breechcloth and then proceeded to paint themselves. An elderly man threw the ball (a small round substance wrapped in deer skin) straight up and the players tried to catch the ball with their ball sticks (or rackets) and throw it to the stakes (goal posts) at opposite ends of the field where points were scored. Games lasted until twilight. Bystanders made their bets ahead of time and often gambled for the clothes they wore.[120]

[August 3, 1811] . . . However, we later heard that the good people[121] were at a ball play on the way to Hightower, where they immediately took their son.[122] It is indescribable how taken the nation is by this ball play, and from year to year it gets worse. No weather is too bad, no road too far! Old and young hurry there, and a ball play is hardly over in *one place* when preparations are made in another.

A true discovery of the enemy—he wants to destroy the minds of the poor people in order to hold them tightly in his ropes! One cannot see without pity how really old people and otherwise truly upstanding people go there with hopes and imagine substantial profits, since it is a betting game. But instead they lose even the shirt off of their backs. It also usually ends in bloody scenes.

[October 1811] *On the 11th* many Indians were here as they also were also several days ago. A ball play was arranged in the neighborhood of the old Vann woman, and Indians from near and far were invited to it. Most of them stopped in here on their way there to quiet their hunger. We would gladly have shown this love to them if they had come in such great numbers for *another* purpose.

Even so, we did not let any of them leave here unsatisfied, but waited on them from early in the morning until into the night. Today, they returned and stopped in again at our place on their way home. Among other guests was also our Johnston with his parents. The boy was, as on his parents' last visit, quite childlike and dear toward us. Toward evening The Tyger,[123] our Dawzizi's father, came very tired and spent the night here. In vain he had looked for his beautiful horse the entire day. After they had beaten him to the ground almost unconscious, three Indians who were completely unknown to him had stolen it from him at the ball play.

Other horses were led away, mistreated in one way or another and made unrecognizable, and then driven into the woods. Oh, it is a quite unholy thing, the ball play here in this country, and the longer the worse! One is just barely over when a new one is arranged.

It is very difficult for us, when it is held close to us, because the Indians who gather for it always stop in here and make our children want to attend it as well.

[July 1812] *On the 11th* Mother Vann visited at our place again and complained to us that some of the Negroes who belong to her daughter Nancy had run away while their mistress was at a ball play. We took the opportunity to speak with her about the futility of all such idle entertainment and to make her aware of the lasting contentment and true rest of the soul. However, she had no ears for this, but even so, she did not seem to take it adversely. This week we had many visits from Indians.

[August 7, 1812] . . . The whole day we had many Indians as guests who were on their way to a large ball play.

On Sunday the 9th, many Indians stopped in at our place on their way back from the ball play.

[October 4, 1812] . . . After we had returned home, Iskittihi, who had formerly run away from our school and considers himself to be great with his silver nose rings, came to our boys and invited them to a ball play in the neighborhood. We were happy that the latter, at our persuasion, immediately dismissed him.

[April 1813] *On the 8th* there was a ball play in our neighborhood again. About thirty Indians stopped in here on their way there. We gladly fed them. However, afterward we learned that they had exerted great effort to talk our boys into going along. But these had excused themselves from this by saying that they do not like to miss their school without important cause and that their learning here was much better and more useful to them than ball play. The Indians knew no words to reply to this.

[May 1813] *On the 29th* John and Dawzizi returned from Harlan's mill,[124] where they had been sent the day before, because the one in our neighborhood was already unusable again. They told us the Indians had tried to talk them into a ball play. However, they had answered them that they took no pleasure in such things, because they were learning something *better* at our place.

[June 1813] *On the 1st* many Indians were here on their way back and forth to a ball play not far from our place. Many spent the night, and some of them slept in the barn.

[August 1813] *On the 28th* we had many visits by Indians, most of whom were on the way to a ball play and the big dance. Among others The Tyger and his wife with two children came to our place to visit their son Dawzizi as well. Our friend The Flea also came. Our houses and barn had to serve as lodging for the many guests.

[June 1815] Early *on the 12th* . . . Jim Foster announced to us that there would be a ball play next Sunday in our vicinity. At our request, Foster promised to use his influence to seek out another place. We considered this as fully the work and effort of the devil to disturb us in our time of quiet and peace in such a way.

[June 1815] Early *on the 17th* there was an *ominous* feeling. Several Indians came in order to inspect the place[125] where ball play was to be held the following day. Brother Hicks took great pains to direct them elsewhere, but in vain.

Quite early *on Sunday the 18th*, many Indians arrived. Brother Hicks again took much trouble to make it plain how improper it was for them to disturb us in our Sunday celebration, but without success. The Tyger, the father of our Dawzizi, was very drunk, and his son had trouble taking him away from here.

Old gray-headed men and women as well as a considerable number of children came with great pomp from all corners and occupied our yard and house so that we were not able to hold our service until two o'clock. . . .

. . . Toward evening, during the Indian's ball play, we held a *Singstunde* without being disturbed. Oh, how sincerely we would wish to experience the time when hundreds of these heathen, who are currently completely blind, might seek the word of salvation in Springplace with the same seriousness we observed today at their gathering for play and come to our worship services in crowds!—No! Even on the most important festival days in the congregation one does not see greater seriousness, zeal, for the services than we saw in these heathen today.

About four o'clock their play began. We were aware of nothing more than several shots and wild screaming, which we heard. At twilight most of them came back. Many went past us quietly. Some of them had gambled away all their valuables, even the clothing off their backs. Several came to demand food and also stayed overnight.

Meanwhile we could not thank our Lord enough that this fearful day passed by safely; He so mercifully prevented us from all harm. Only The Tyger made trouble and difficulty for his son throughout the night. He threatened to beat his good wife[126] and little son,[127] who had taken refuge with us. Finally Dawzizi convinced him with friendly and serious words to go with him to Vann's plantation, where he entrusted him to a Negro to watch over him.

At night he came again as well as two other drunken people, who woke us with loud screaming under our door, which was half open on account of the great heat, and cried to Sister Gambold to give them apples. Immediately Dawzizi was there and gave them what they demanded and led them along with his father to the place in the woods where the play had been, and where there were several in the same circumstances as they.

Early *on the 19th*, the Brethren Gambold[128] went out in order to see whether damage had occurred in our new cornfield but found none. We thanked our dear Lord truly for this. Meanwhile, at the ball play grounds, which looked like a battlefield, they found about thirty Indians, some still very badly injured and covered with blood, and some drunk.

Our hearts still ached and now fervent sighs for the salvation of these miserable heathens rose to the *Redeemer of the World.*

The Tyger also returned and demanded food, and when it was offered to him, he would not take it; rather, he drank only a little milk.[129] Nevertheless, he was quiet and peaceful. It seemed to touch his heart that his son was very helpful in the mother's escape and had accompanied her to Sister Peggy's.[130]

He addressed him in the following manner: "You concern yourself very much about Mother, but you abandon me to stand alone like a dog," etc. With eyes full of tears, the boy's answer was, "Father, I must protect my mother from you, when you are drunk. I love you as much, but your behavior hurts me. There is nothing I want as much as for you but to abstain totally from drinking brandy," etc. At this his father seemed touched and was silent.

We took advantage of the opportunity to speak with the mother about her son's intention to live entirely with us. "Oh," she said, "he has my complete approval. Here he is in good hands. At home he would become a drunkard just like his father." The son himself translated all of this for us.

Otherwise The Tyger and his wife live together on the best terms, and they are very diligent people. His strong passion for brandy, however, causes his good-natured wife grief. Numerous Indians gradually appeared to be fed.

[June 1816] *On the 1st* . . . . The Tyger, his brother-in-law, and two other Indians came for tomorrow's ball play in our neighborhood.

. . . We celebrated undisturbed through heathen noises from our neighborhood, even with the usual all-night dance that was associated with ball play. . . .

To our distress, on Whitsuntide, *Sunday the 2nd*, we could not have our morning service because up to the time set for the ball play, our houses were full of Indians, among whom we found relatives of our students. There was a melancholy feeling and we could do nothing except quietly commend these poor blinded heathens to the compassionate Savior. . . .

. . . In the evening Watie came back from the ball play and stayed overnight here.

[June 1817] *On Sunday the 29th* . . . There were no Negroes present; the overseer and they were absent, unfortunately. They amused themselves at ball play. It was very loud.

[August 1817] *On the 6th* between school sessions, we found our children at ball play with a few Indians in our lane. In the presence of Indians, they were called in for very serious accounting. A few appeared remorseful. However, Buck remained difficult, and he troubled us greatly.

[September 1817] *On the 17th* many travelers came in and also many Indians on their way to a ball play. Three of them spent the night.

On Sunday the 21st . . . Many Indians on their way to a *general ball play* poured in from all corners and borders of the nation to Coosawattee, traveled by here, and entered our mission. A few came to our spring to find a root[131] that is supposed to bring a ball player success and good luck. Also the Negroes from our neighborhood were invited; the nightlong dance was held this evening. However, we did not let it disturb our Holy Communion; rather, we commended the oppressive feeling around us to the sweet nearness of our dear Savior for a blessed sleep.

On the 22nd, since great threats had been issued against our Brother Crutchfield on part of the enemy, various friends and finally Brother Hicks had informed him, namely, that it had been rumored the wicked attack would have been executed on the return trip from ball play.[132]

On the 23rd, since this was the day intended for the attack on Brother Crutchfield, the texts for the day were unusually comforting to us. Our Brother was also truly calm and not frightened. The threat remained unfulfilled,[133] and everyone went quietly home. God be praised!

[January 1818] *On the 21st* Dawzizi, who had gone to help his relatives for some days, returned and informed us that his father had promised him he should have permission in the fall to go wherever he wanted, if he would stay with him the next summer. He also said his father would now stop talking him into attending the ball play because he agreed that all his efforts were in vain.

[August 24, 1818] . . . This evening there was a dance and a horrible clamor as a preparation for a ball play just at the entrance to our lane by the big spring. In our evening service we prayed for the poor people and felt our dear Savior's presence in our midst.

In the afternoon *on the 25th*, Dawzizi's parents, brother,[134] and relatives went to the ball play. He and his young brother,[135] however, stayed with us.

In the afternoon *on the 27th*, Dawzizi's mother returned from the ball play. His father had stayed behind in a drinking company. Our neighbor Joseph Vann had arranged this game and had already practiced for it with his faction for two weeks in the hope of winning it. However, the opposite happened to him.

[July 4, 1819] Afterward, because a ball play had been arranged in the neighborhood, our friend The Little Broom asked us for some magic corals which they believe help them to find out which party will win. Brother and Sister Vann told us that in the morning their neighbors had invited one of their Negroes and their granddaughter Ruth Falling to go to the game. *They*, however, had sent the messenger away and told him that no one from their family should attend any more such heathen entertainment. Afterward, we talked for a long time with them and Sister Crutchfield.

[April 30, 1820]: . . . However, toward evening we experienced the very deeply felt pain of learning from Misses Russell and McCartney, who had gone to their house, that they had met our boys in a ball play with the Negroes. After evening devotion, we emphatically explained to them this sinful and extremely insolent behavior of theirs, in its greatness and consequences not only to our pain but even more to our dear Savior's pain.

[August 6, 1820] . . . In spite of our repeated warnings, some of our pupils sneaked away from here at every opportunity to entertain themselves in ball play with Joseph Vann's Negroes. Just yesterday we had a sad example, so Brother Gambold used the sermon as an opportunity to speak especially to them, through the goodness to which they daily are invited by the Savior. He used the sermon to show that the Savior also wants to gather them under His wings of grace. He, however, would have to say *to them* with pain and sorrow, "You have not desired it until now." During this they were asked quite urgently even now, while it is still today, to reflect on what will lead to their peace.

On the 7th we had the pain of noting that this did not have the desired result, when two of the eldest announced that they wanted to go home for a while. Since we are expecting the parents of both here on the 13th of this month, we told them to be patient until then, when we would tell their parents ourselves of their desire and the true reason for this. This made them very downcast.

[July 1821] *On the 19th* the Indians had a large dance and ball play about eight miles from here.

On the 20th we received many visits from those who were returning from the dance, and we had to feed them.

[August 1821] *On the 4th*, all at once, four of our pupils were fetched home for a visit, which we found strange. We learned later that there will be a ball play for children in Sumach Town.

On the 5th about sixty children gathered there for this purpose. However, when the playing was supposed to begin, they were afraid of each other, and all attempts by the older ones to convince them to play were in vain. They had to separate again without accomplishing their purpose.

[October 1821] *On the 25th* we[136] went to the Council House, where we heard old Chief Pathkiller give a talk. During the talk, some old men went around the circle with tobacco pipes, and each person took a couple of puffs. It was also offered to us as a sign of friendship. After the gathering, we greeted all the chiefs who were especially friendly to Brother Gambold, whom they consider their faithful friend of many years. Old Chief Gentleman Tom told Brother Gambold, "When I visited you in your house at the Springs, I always got enough to eat and also tobacco to smoke, and that was good." To this Brother Gambold replied that he had always enjoyed it when he visited and that this Brother[137] of his who was standing next to him would be just as happy if he visited him and he would always accept him with the same friendship and hospitality. While he shook our hands he said "Osio," "That is good."

There was ball play here every day and Indian dances in the evening to watch around a great fire to in front of the Council House.

Cherokee Origin Stories

Uniluchfty's and The Elk's[138] *storytelling held rich and significant information concerning the way early nineteenth century Cherokees authenticated their universe and promoted views they believed essential, really very essential, to their survival. Linda Tuhiwai Smith in* Decolonizing Methodologies: Research and Indigenous Peoples *defines the concept of essentialism from the Native view, contending that human relationships are based on a shared "essence" of life. The essence of a person can be traced back to an earth parent; the essence of a person has a genealogy. A human person also projects a sense of spirituality whereby animate and inanimate beings or objects share the same spiritual realms. Lastly, the significance of place, of land, of landscape, of other things in the universe, all define what essentialism means to Native Peoples.*[139]

Uniluchfty

[May 1810] *On Sunday the 20th* . . . In the afternoon an old Indian named Uniluchfty very graciously offered us his hand and said that the last time he was here, we had told him we would be happy to see him again. He was old and his hearing was bad. Often he remembered, however, that we told him if the *Great Man* in the sky lets us live a long time, then we become *old.*

We were very happy to have Mrs. Vann with us just then, because we wanted to discuss various things with this man, whom *she* also knows as an upright Indian. We had him asked how his health was. Answer: "I have *never* been sick; therefore, I expect if I ever become ill, then I will die." This provided an opportunity to talk with him about the immortality of the soul and its blessed or wretched condition after death.

Whereupon he said that he remembered *well* that we had told him such words during his last visit here. He had thought a lot about this and had also discussed it sometimes until late in the night with Mr. Charles Hicks since he lives in his neighborhood.[140] He also never goes to sleep without first having talked with God. But he does not know *much*, because the Indians in general know little of God and do not have books or fitting words for prayer.

We told him that God sees the heart and not the *words*. He replied that he knew well that there were two paths, one to *evil* and the other to *goodness*. We, however, knew the right way, which leads to *goodness*. We tried to show him this as clearly as possible in his language with the help of Mrs. Vann. Silently, however, we sighed quite frankly, "Oh dear Savior, show Yourself to him as the Way, the Truth, and the Life, without Whom no one comes to the Father!"

Mrs. Vann then told him the story about the creation of the world, the first humans, their fall, and its unblessed consequences for all of their descendants and that God's Son came down from heaven in order to redeem this fall. He became a child, lived on the earth, suffered for us, and was finally crucified, buried, and resurrected. He went to heaven where He now lives and rules eternally, and after their death, He will also take to Himself all, after death, who believe that He shed His blood for *them* and who thankfully accept His salvation.

He sat there deep in thought. After a while, he said that the old Indians also had confused ideas about the creation of humans. The Great Man in the sky had first laid two pieces of stone next to each other and covered them with a deerskin. After seven nights he looked to see if they were moving. Since he found them lifeless, however, he laid two balls of clay in their place and covered them with the deerskin again.

After seven nights, he actually found these in motion. Two *children* were created this way, who later, when they were grown, became our first parents. When these new creatures were seen by a ground squirrel, a frog, and an earthworm, the three consulted about what to do with them. The ground squirrel said, "After seven nights they should die, because it is their fault that I have seven stripes on my back." The frog said, "Yes, they should die, because they pressed my head flat!" The earthworm, however, was incensed at these words, writhed impatiently, and finally left entirely. Since he did not want to agree to their suggestions, the two humans were left living.

He had also heard about the fall of man, but not, as one can well imagine, according to the truth. He said that some Indians, especially the old ones, at least knew that if our first parents had not been *bad*, their descendants would have a much better life. They would be served by bears instead of pigs, by buffaloes instead of cattle, and by elk instead of horses.

The Elk

[October 1815] *On the 13th* an extraordinary number of Indians came here on their way to the agency. Among them we saw a few of our friends whom we have not seen for three years. We deemed it necessary to dismiss our school in order to prepare food for them and to serve them by writing.[141] Among those who demanded the latter from us was an old chief named The Elk from Pine Log; by all appearances, he was a very poor man who comported himself *very importantly*, as if he had to express business of very great consequence to the agent.[142] None of our children was able to serve him as translator. *Everyone* assured him they did not understand what he said. We knew no advice to give. Then we could not refuse him since he thought his reasons seemed of the greatest importance. At his urgent request, Brother Gambold finally agreed to go with him to Mountjoy in order to get his message through our Peggy even though he heard she had already declined to do this for him before. He had made his pressing case. All protests in this intent were in vain, and Brother Gambold was obliged to write the following message to Colonel Meigs: "You[143] said at Tuckabatchie,[144] the white people desired *more* land from the Indians: now I will inform you of our ancestry.

"At first there was a man and a woman on the earth.[145] They had two sons, who made an attempt on the life of their mother on the pretext that she was a sorceress because she procured sufficient food for them without planting and they could not discover where she got it. And this was her way: she went out and quickly returned with the necessary provisions. The bad intentions[146] of the sons against the mother was finally found out, and she talked this over with them and requested they stop, because she would not stay with them much longer but would go into the sky; they would never see her again.

"However, she would attentively watch all of their behavior. If they resolved to be *evil,* gloom would surround them. Soon thereafter she left her sons and quickly rose into the heights. The father was not home at that time. When he came home, he expressed his displeasure at his sons' conduct toward their mother, and he admonished them to improve themselves.

"He handed them a book from which they should learn trade and commerce.[147] The first son forcefully snatched the book away and ran away from his father's house with it. The father, before he went upward, drew a line between the two brothers and their dwelling places. This line is the sea. Now the two brothers discovered a great deal of pleasure playing in the water; that one who possessed the book remained on the other side, and the other brother who stayed at the father's house lived on this side. They took canoes and followed the course of the sun that they perceived as always setting in the sea.

"Finally, King George from the other side of the line made great boats, and his people followed the same course of the sun until they finally came to the land on this side. In these great boats, King George sent his brothers gifts. These brothers were entirely naked, and the first brother still lived. But he was old and not in the position to walk as quickly as the young people, who grabbed all these gifts and kept them only for themselves.

"I, The Elk, am certainly a descendant from the family of the first inhabitants this side of the sea in the seventh generation! The brothers *from this side* of the sea were originally *white* as those from the other side, but they did not take the same care to protect themselves against the sun. And I am the only man in the nation who knows this." Oh, how Brother Gambold heartily sighed that the eyes and ears of this poor blinded heathen would open so that he would learn God's Word as the *Truth.* His and Peggy's efforts were solely in vain. He and his companions sat there fully caught in a wind and firmly resolute that no one should take away their beliefs.

Cherokees' Responses to Christian Images

Once Indians walked across the Moravian mission's threshold, they discovered a people, though highly regimented in their own Christian rituals, willing to record Indian worldview. Similarly, colonial historian James P. Ronda has illuminated seventeenth-century interaction of Jesuits and Indians and has argued that genuine theological debates transpired between Indian sachems and missionaries. Ronda noted that when Montagnais shaman Carigonon and Jesuit priest Le Jeune discussed their beliefs in the afterlife, neither agreed with the other, but their exchanges revealed that they both had a belief in the supernatural and its interaction with man. When Le Jeune left the Montagnais, he admitted that the Indians maintained their faith as "tenaciously as did any pious Christian."[148]

Likewise, most Cherokees neither converted to Christianity nor desired to abandon the Indian sense of the transcendental, mystic, and monistic. Rather, the Moravians' presence challenged Cherokee curiosity about Moravian spirituality and provoked Cherokee interest in Moravian beliefs. For example, Cherokee exposure to Moravian religious artifacts such as pictures of the crucifix, Virgin Mary, and the Baby Jesus prompted Cherokee visitors like The Little Broom, The Bird, and The Flea to comment on Christian images. Inadvertently, Cherokees' remarks to Moravian explanations led to deeper understandings of early nineteenth-century Cherokee spirituality. However, their interaction was one of "contest," describing what ethnohistorian James Axtell calls primarily a conflict "between two concepts of spiritual power and the quality of life each offered."[149]

The Little Broom

[October 1815] *On the 12th* . . . The Tyger, The Little Broom, and his wife ate the noon meal with us. They meditated on the picture of the crucifixion of our Savior. Dawzizi explained to them the important and several necessary truths. His father listened thoughtfully, but The Little Broom laughed really loud in an Indian manner, as if it meant something new and strange to them.

The Flea

[December 1807] Early in the day *on the 29th* . . . Our children told us that The Flea and his wife really wanted to attend a service here. We had them come to our place in the evening and sang our Christmas Psalm,[150] during which the two old people sat with folded hands in great reverence. When the Psalm was over, The Flea said that his heart was very touched by our singing, and he wished he could also sing. We told him that God saw the heart's desire as a fact.

Then he relayed that God had appeared to him in his youth, apparently in a dream. He looked just as friendly and nice as this person, pointing to the Virgin Mary, and was wearing silver, very brightly gleaming clothes. He added that he knew very little about God, but as often as he thinks about Him, he has a very good feeling in his heart. He at least knows that God takes those who love him on earth to Himself in heaven after their death. The evil ones, however, He sends to an evil place, and this earth will also one day burn up with fire. With this we took the opportunity to talk with him about our Savior's humiliation, life, sufferings, and death, out of love for humanity in order to redeem everyone from eternal fear and suffering. During this the children showed him the picture of the Baby Jesus, which pleased him so much that he could hardly take his eyes from it. Finally we told him that he should imagine God as pure love when he thinks about Him and never forget that nothing but love drove Him to become a human child and to die for us.

Also that His heavenly Father loved men with equal love, because He let Him come to us in this world out of pure love. We could not tell how the children explained this to these dear people in their inadequate language. This much, however, is true, that both of them seemed to be very moved, and The Flea repeatedly cried out, "Osio! Osio!"[151] and smiled in a very friendly manner. We all felt unusually well during this.

Early in the day *on the 30th*, The Flea came back to Brother and Sister Gambold's house to see the Baby Jesus once more. It was strange that the picture of young John the Baptist, which was put up across from the other one of the manger scene and was just as big, did not please him as much or even more. Despite the effort the children made to draw his attention to it, and the fact that John's bright clothing was much more attractive to an Indian eye than the Baby Jesus, who was wrapped in rags, nonetheless, he took no notice of this picture. Finally he said that he would really like to own a picture of God so young. He did not want it under glass, but simply on paper so that he could look at it daily. We explained to him that we did not have another one here at this time, but if we should later get one, we would let him have it. He seemed to be completely satisfied with this.

Then he asked to see the children in their school routine. We gathered them together and had them sing, pray, and read. He was very pleased and had the children tell us that he always had a good feeling in his heart when he was in our company.

The Bird

[December 1808] *On the 15th* . . . In the afternoon a chief, named *The Bird*, arrived here and attended our Passion Liturgy in the evening. The children told us that they had already told him much about the birth, life, sufferings, death, resurrection, and ascension of our dear Lord; he wants to hear more about this. Then we then told him the story of the creation of the world, the first man and his fall, the unhappiness that came to all humans as a result of this, and the necessity of the Redeemer.

With warm hearts we told him about the love of God for his poor fallen humans, who prevailed upon Him *alone* to have mercy on us, to suffer in our place, to atone for our sins, and to pay with His blood. He sat there deep in thought. Finally he asked if He shed *all* of His blood. And did it fall onto the earth? We answered affirmatively and spoke further about this great matter. Then he asked, "Who had made *God*?"

We answered that God had always been here, that He tells us this in

His book, which He left behind; it tells us about His love and His whole existence and will. . . .

. . . He seemed to be very taken in by these matters, and at his request, the children talked with him about the love of our Lord until late in the night.

In the morning *on the 17th*, the admirable old chief very cordially left and added that he would often think about what he had heard from us, so that he would not forget it.

Epilogue

As Cherokees transcended the deceits and vagaries of the Early Republic's assimilation or "civilization" Indian policies, they became increasingly under pressure to cede land in the East and move west. One Cherokee family, the Ridges, was extraordinarily affected by the "civilization program." As noted earlier, John Ridge wrote to President James Monroe in 1821 of his parents' desire to have their children educated. He noted that although his parents were "ignorant of the *English Language*, but it is astonishing to see them exert all their power to have their Children educated like the whites."[1]

Many Cherokees like the Ridges proved their willingness to assimilate in order to maintain their homeland; they had accepted missionaries to educate their children and Indian agents to dispense western-style farming equipment and livestock. Furthermore, Cherokees adopted a republican government in 1828 with the election of John Ross as principal chief, reflecting their nationhood and identity within the United States. But becoming "civilized" was not enough for Andrew Jackson and his constituency. As Elias Boudinot, cousin of John Ridge, remarked: "[A] desire to possess the Indian Land is paramount to a desire to see him established on the soil as a civilized man."[2]

Contentiousness over Cherokee ancestral domains permeated Cherokees' souls and prompted others around them to contemplate their future in their hereditary lands. This epilogue, like the rest of this abridgment, uses narratives or parts of narratives to give voice to the Cherokees.

John Gambold's own dissatisfaction with the Tennessee governor was clear as he wrote that "the [U.S.] government is certainly disposed in a fatherly way to this poor nation, but it has appointed men who are ignorant of the Indians and whose hearts are not warm with love for their poor neighbors. Governor McMinn of Tennessee is striving hard to promote the emigration of the Cherokees as much as possible. He is very concerned that at least in the part of land which will eventually be given to Tennessee, as few Indians as possible get reserves because such reserves would provide no income for his state in the sale of the land. He is said to have expressed himself very harshly against Mr. Cornelius[3] and Mr. Kingsbury[4] and even threatened to lock them up if they continue to persuade the Indian to hold on to their land, how this was reported to them about him, I do not know on what grounds."[5]

Meanwhile, Cherokees continued to thwart threats of removal, and they retained most of their ancestral domain until forced removal in 1838–39. In the 1820s Moravian missionary Johannes Renatus Schmidt, who replaced John Gambold, sensed that he should refrain from allowing Moravian records to reveal Cherokee resolve to practice and sustain Cherokee traditions in their lands. In 1824 Schmidt observed that "this [is the] time not to reveal the particulars about Cherokee society: . . . if this is printed and read in the country then it could be seen as if people wanted to put the Nation in bad light, especially since they have already been made to believe that they are an uncivilized people."[6]

Notes

Editorial Policy

1. The editorial policy for this abridgment follows the policy set for *The Moravian Springplace Mission to the Cherokees*, xv–xxii.

2. Julian P. Boyd, "'God's Altar Need Not Our Pollishings'" in *New York History* 39, no. 1 (January 1958): 3–21.

3. Tiya A. Miles has written *The House on Diamond Hill: A Cherokee Plantation Story* (Chapel Hill: University of North Carolina Press, 2010) on Cherokee slaveholding and Vann slavery. Information about Vann slavery has been extracted from *The Moravian Springplace Mission to the Cherokees.*

Introduction

1. I am using Craig Atwood's historical understanding and application of the term *Brüdergemeine* from his *Community of the Cross: Moravian Piety in Colonial Bethlehem*, Max Kade German American Research Institute Series (University Park: Pennsylvania State University Press, 2004). I use the terms *Brüdergemeine* and Moravian interchangeably.

2. For the most recent study of Springplace Mission and the roles of Cherokee and Moravian women, in particular Anna Rosina's, see Anna Smith, "Unlikely Sisters: Cherokee and Moravian Women in the Early Nineteenth Century," in *Pious Pursuits: German Moravians in the Atlantic World*, ed. Michele Gillespie and Robert Beachy (New York: Berghahn Books, 2007), 191–206.

3. Frederick A. Cook, Larry D. Brown, and Jack E. Oliver, "The Southern

Appalachians and the Growth of Continents," *Scientific American* 243 (October 1980): 163–65; Albert E. Cowdry, *The Land, This South: An Environmental History* (Lexington: University Press of Kentucky, 1983), 1; Timothy Silver, *The New Age of the Countryside: Indian, Colonists, and Slaves in South Atlantic Forest, 1500–1800* (Cambridge: Cambridge University Press, 1990), 10–12; William Cronon, *Changes in the Land: Indians, Colonists, and the Ecology of New England* (New York: Hill and Wang, 1996); Alfred W. Crosby, *Ecological Imperialism: The Biological Expansion of Europe, 900–1900* (Cambridge: Cambridge University Press, 1986)

4. John Melish, *The Traveller's Directory through the United States* (Philadelphia: T. H. Palmer, 1819), 32.

5. See also the following works that entail Moravian missionary work from 1735 to 1821: Adelaide L. Fries, *Moravians in Georgia, 1735–1740* (Raleigh NC: Edwards and Broughton, 1905); John Heckewelder, *Narrative of the Missions of the United Brethren among the Delaware and Mohegan Indians, from its Commencement, in the Year 1740, to the Close in the Year, 1808* (Philadelphia: McCarthy and Davis, 1820; reprint, Arno Press and New York Times, 1971); Jane T. Merritt, "Dreaming of the Savior's Blood: Moravians and the Indian Great Awakening in Pennsylvania," *William and Mary Quarterly* 54 (1997): 723–46; Linda Sabathy-Judd, *Moravians in Upper Canada: The Fairfield Diary, 1792–1813* (Toronto: Champlain Society, 1999); Amy C. Schutt, *Peoples of the River Valleys: The Odyssey of the Delaware Indians* (Philadelphia: University of Pennsylvania Press, 2007); Corinna Dally-Starna and William A. Starna, "American Indians and Moravians in Southern New England" in *Germans and Indians: Fantasies, Encounters, Projections*, ed. Colin G. Calloway, Gerd Gemünden, and Susanne Zantrop (Lincoln: University of Nebraska Press, 2002); Carola Wessel, *Delaware-Indianer und Herrnhuter Missionare im Upper Ohio Valley, 1772–1781*, Hallesche Forschungen, 4 (Tübingen: Verlag der Franckeschen Stiftungen Halle im Max Niemeyer Verlag, 1999), 267–88, 311–44; and Hermann Wellenreuter and Wessel, *Herrnhuter Indianermission in der Amerikanishchen Revolution: Die Tagesbücher von David Zeisberger 1772 bis 1781* (Berlin: Akademie Verlag, 1995).

For studies of interracial cooperation with emphasis on settler expansion creating a racially tense landscape, refer to Jane T. Merritt, *At the Crossroads: Indians and Empires on a Mid-Atlantic Frontier, 1700–1763* (Chapel Hill: University of North Carolina Press, 2003). Chapter 4, "Mission Community Network," entails a study of Moravian mission communities among the Mahicans and Delawares.

Recent publications pertaining to eighteenth-century Moravian mission work among Natives are: Katherine Cartè Engel, *Religion and Profit: Moravians in Early America* (Philadelphia: University of Pennsylvania Press, 2009); Schutt, *Peoples of the River Valleys*; Corinna Dally-Starna and William A. Starna, ed. and trans.,

Gideon's People, 2 vols. (Lincoln: University of Nebraska Press, 2009); the English translation, Carola Wessel and Hermann Wellenreuter, eds., *The Moravian Mission Diaries of David Zeisberger* (University Park: Pennsylvania State University Press, 2005); and Rachel Wheeler, *To Live upon Hope: Mohicans and Missionaries in the Eighteenth-Century Northeast* (Ithaca NY: Cornell University Press, 2008).

6. Edmund Schwarze, *History of the Moravian Missions among Southern Indian Tribes of the United States* (1923; reprint, Grove OK: Stauber Books, 1999), 65.

7. For further information on the Federal Road, see E. Raymond Evans "Highways to Progress: Nineteenth-Century Roads in the Cherokee Nation," *Journal of Cherokee Studies* 2, no. 4 (Fall 1977): 394–400; and John H. Goff, "Retracing the Old Federal Road," *Georgia Mineral News Letter* 10, no. 4 (Winter 1957): n.p. Note: When finished, the road's "spur" went to Tellico.

8. Kenneth G. Hamilton, trans. and ed., "Minutes of the Mission Conference Held in Springplace," *Atlanta Historical Bulletin* 16 (Spring 1971): 51; and Schwarze, *History of the Moravian Missions*, 134.

9. James Vann was born in 1768; his exact heritage is uncertain. His mother was Cherokee, a member of the Blind Savannah clan. His father first built a trading post near the Chattahoochee River and then moved this post further into the Cherokee Nation near the Conasauga River. By 1809 this area became known as Vannsville, but in the early 1800s Vann in his correspondence refers to the area as Diamond Hill. William G. McLoughlin, "James Vann: Intemperate Patriot, 1768–1809," in *The Cherokee Ghost Dance: Essays on the Southeastern Indians, 1789–1861* (Macon GA: Mercer University Press, 1984), 39–72; and Whitfield-Murray Historical Society, *Murray County's Indian Heritage* (1987; reprint, Fernandina Beach,FL: Wolfe Publishing, 1997), 3.

10. Doublehead, a Lower Town Chief, was assassinated in 1807 for selling part of the Cherokee Nation for personal gain in the 1806 Treaty of Washington. Walter Lowrie, Walter S. Franklin, and Matthew St. Clair Clark, eds., *American State Papers: Indian Affairs, Documents, Legislative and Executive, of the Congress of the United States* (Washington DC: Gales and Seaton, 1832, 1834), 2:146, 147; and McLoughlin, *Cherokee Renascence in the New Republic* (Princeton NJ: Princeton University Press, 1986), 115, 158, 192, 238–39, 254. See also Francis Paul Prucha, *American Indian Policy in the Formative Years: The Trade and Intercourse Acts, 1790–1834* (Cambridge MA: Harvard University Press, 1962), 226, 227; and Thurman Wilkins, *Cherokee Tragedy: The Story of the Ridge Family and of the Decimation of a People* (1970; reprint, Norman: University of Oklahoma Press, 1986), 39–41.

11. Little Turkey was principal chief of the Lower Towns.

12. The drawing of "the lot" (signaled by an asterisk in Moravian manuscripts), an ancient church practice resurrected in 1728 by Count Nicholas Ludwig

von Zinzendorf, assured communicants that Christ, not humankind, made all decisions including who would be chosen for membership, who would receive membership privileges (baptism and communion), where to establish missions, and members' marriage partners and occupations. Thus the lot determined the Vann site. Schwarze, *History of the Moravian Missions*, 56–59. The lot decided the fate of every individual. Pieces of paper marked "*Ja*" or "*Nein*," or left blank, were put in a box. If a spiritual leader drew a blank, it meant the decision was deferred. The lot managed almost every detail of congregational life. The church used this arbitrary system not only to assign persons to various positions in the community, but also to determine community policy, accept new arrivals into the community, and change professions. When Moravians went into the mission field, the lot settled questions involving whether to accept Indian converts into baptism, what to name mission outposts, whether to abandon old settlements, and where to settle the Indians in Christian missions. The Moravians often sought spiritual guidance directly from Christ, believing that He would answer their sincere prayers in the drawing of lots. C. Daniel Crews, *Moravian Meanings: A Glossary of Historical Terms of the Moravian Church, Southern Province* (reprint, Winston-Salem NC: Moravian Archives, 1996), 18.

13. Schwarze, *History of the Moravian Missions*, 55, 58.

14. In 1792 the Washington administration established Fort Southwest Point at the confluence of the Clinch and Tennessee rivers to maintain peace between settlers and Indians. In 1801 Colonel Return Jonathan Meigs as Cherokee Indian agent moved to Southwest Point and fortified it. In 1807 he relocated his headquarters to Hiwassee Garrison, at the confluence of the Hiwassee and Tennessee rivers. Luke H. Banker, "Fort Southwest Point, Tennessee: The Development of a Frontier Post, 1792–1807" (master's thesis, University of Tennessee, 1972), ii, 3–4.

15. Meigs, a Revolutionary War hero with the rank of colonel, was a native of Connecticut and sixty-one years old when he came to Cherokee territory in 1801 as United States Indian agent to the Cherokees. Though "scrupulously honest" with money that passed through his hands, about five hundred thousand dollars in his twenty-two years of service to the Cherokee Nation, he persevered in pressuring the Cherokees to cede land in the east for land in the west. William G. McLoughlin, "Who Civilized the Cherokees?" *Journal of Cherokee Studies* 13 (1988): 63, 64; James Sean McKeown, "Return J. Meigs: United States Agent in the Cherokee Nation, 1801–1823" (PhD diss., Pennsylvania State University, 1984); and Henry Thompson Malone, "Return Jonathan Meigs: Indian Agent Extraordinary," *East Tennessee Historical Society's Publications*, no. 28 (1956); and Robert Sparks Walker, *Torchlights to the Cherokees* (New York: Macmillan, 1931; reprint, Johnson City TN: Overmountain Press, 1993), 88.

16. Doublehead referred to Upper Town Cherokee leader James Vann. Correspondence, John and Anna Rosina Gambold to the Provincial Helper's Conference in Salem, October 26, 1805, Moravian Archives, Salem (hereafter cited as MAS).

17. Early Republic leaders reasoned that continuing Indian wars would be costly to the new nation. Washington's Indian policy, under the Department of War, fostered the concept of beneficent imperialism toward Indians. The president and secretary of war Henry Knox wanted the new government to replace the Confederation's Indian policy of conquest, which had denied treaty rights and rightful Indian ownership of land, with a "civilization" program that would promote Indian rights to lands they cultivated, peaceful acculturation, and quiet white expansion. The Washington administration believed posterity would judge it benign toward Indians if it displayed such imperial beneficence, so it introduced the "clean hands policy." Various Trade and Intercourse Acts, passed between 1790 and 1823, included philanthropic measures such as paying missionaries to live among the Native peoples to Christianize them and educate them in the European sense. This plan supposedly would make Indians not only predictable but less reticent to preserve ancestral landholdings. U.S. policy makers encouraged male Indians, who had been hunters and meat producers, to vacate the hunt and become agriculturalists, traditionally belonging to the female realm, and substitute digging sticks for the plow and oxen. They demanded that women embrace republican womanhood, abandoning agricultural production to become cloth weavers and keepers of the hearth. Reginald Horsman, *Expansion and American Indian Policy, 1783–1812* (1967, Norman: University of Oklahoma, reprint, 1992), 53–83. For discussions of early U.S. philanthropic gestures toward Indians and their questionable benefits, see Bernard Sheehan, *Seeds of Extinction: Jeffersonian Philanthropy and the American Indian* (Chapel Hill: University of North Carolina Press, 1973). The late scholar and researcher Wilbur R. Jacobs argues that Sheehan's interpretations are difficult and that his conclusion may leave the reader unconvinced that "Jeffersonian philanthropists were consistently motivated by benevolent ideals" (604). Jacobs, "Native American History: How It Illuminates Our Past," *American Historical Review* 80 (June 1975): 595–609. For agreement with Sheehan and general praise of his work, see Francis Paul Prucha, "Note: Books on American Indian Policy: A Half-Decade of Important Work, 1970–1975," *Journal of American History* 63 (December 1976): 658–69. Prucha claims that Sheehan's text is a necessary and "welcomed balance to other writings" which depict only white ruthlessness (662).

18. A *Lebenslauf* (Memoir or Life's Journey) was not prepared for Anna Rosina Gambold, so very little information has surfaced so far about her early life in Bethlehem. Her parents were Daniel Kliest (1716–1792), an experienced

locksmith, and Anna Felicitas née Schuster (1729–1757); they married October 4, 1757. Daniel's first wife, Anna Rosina née Beyer, died December 9, 1750. In 1752 the Moravian Church sent Daniel to serve as a missionary in Shekomeko (Dutchess County, New York), where he stated that he "loved them from my heart, and they loved me also" (translated by author). Daniel Kliest, *Lebenslauf*, Moravian Archives, Bethlehem (hereafter cited as MAB). See also Engel, *Religion and Profit*, 150, 203.

19. Moravian scholars have coined the term "sifting" or "winnowing" to describe a time of Moravian fanaticism that lasted until 1750. However, Moravian records indicate that in outlying settlements such as the Springplace Mission vestiges of sifting lingered well into the nineteenth century. The term "sifting" referred to the Bible verse in Luke in which Jesus told Simon Peter he would be tempted by Satan: "And the Lord said, Simon, Simon, behold Satan hath desired to have you, that he may sift you as wheat" (Luke 22:31). Daniel B. Thorp, *The Moravian Community in Colonial North Carolina: Pluralism in Colonial America* (Knoxville: University of Tennessee Press, 1989), 22.

20. Beverly Prior Smaby, *The Transformation of Moravian Bethlehem from Communal Mission to Family Economy* (Philadelphia: University of Pennsylvania Press, 1988), 10–13. See also chapter 5, "Life Cycles and Values," 145–95, for a discussion of Bethlehem choirs.

21. For a discussion of the Single Sisters' Choir, see Smaby, "Forming the Single Sisters' Choir in Bethlehem," *Transactions of the Moravian Historical Society* 28 (1994): 1–14; and Smaby, *Transformation of Moravian Bethlehem*, 36, 37. After 1762 the Bethlehem community kept the choirs for Widows, Widowers, Single Sisters, and Single Brethren.

22. Jacob John Sessler, *Communal Pietism among Early American Moravians* (New York: Henry Holt, 1933), 96–99.

23. Sessler, *Communal Pietism*, 96–99. An example of Married Men's and Women's Choir buildings still stands in the Moravian section of Bethlehem, on Church Street. In earlier Moravian settlements such as Bethlehem, Moravians had conjugal rights but otherwise husband and wife lived apart in separate dwellings.

24. Gillian Lindt Gollin, *Moravians in Two Worlds: A Study of Changing Communities* (New York: Columbia University Press, 1967), 67–89.

25. Historically, the appellations Brother and Sister were given to Moravian communicants. Arthur J. Freeman, *An Ecumenical Theology of the Heart: The Theology of Count Nicholas Ludwig von Zinzendorf* (Bethlehem PA: Moravian Church in America, 1998), 4.

26. After 1762, Moravians began to live as husband and wife in the same house,

but the choir houses remained for the unmarried single men and women and the widowers and widows. For a comprehensive study of communal Bethlehem, see Smaby, *Transformation of Moravian Bethlehem.*

27. Elizabeth Lehman Myers, *A Century of Moravian Sisters: A Record of Christian Community Life* (New York: Fleming H. Revell, 1918), 39, 40–44, 91.

28. Myers, *Century of Moravian Sisters*, 22.

29. "Speakings," or *Sprechen*, were interviews about one's spiritual life and fitness that every communicant was required to have prior to Holy Communion. These "speakings" did not resemble confessions; rather, they allowed the communicant to confide in the spiritual leader the condition of his or her heart and to have "soul searching" conversations. Crews, *Moravian Meanings*, 29.

30. Before Zinzendorf's death in 1760, fourteen women were ordained as priestesses, but after 1760 there were none.

31. Anna Rosina Gambold had a picture of the Virgin Mary at Springplace; frequent Cherokee visitor The Flea pointed to the picture as a reminder of his memory of God.

32. Katherine M. Faull, introduction to *Moravian Women's Memoirs: Their Related Lives, 1750–1820* (Syracuse NY: Syracuse University Press, 1997), xxvii–xxxi, xxxv.

33. Faull, *Moravian Women's Memoirs*, 136; and Erich Beyreuther, "Ehe-Religion und Eschaton" in *Studien zur Theologie Zinzendorfs* (Neukirchen: Neukirchener Verlag, 1962), 53–73.

34. William C. Reichel, *A History of the Rise, Progress, and Present Condition of the Bethlehem Seminary with a Catalogue of Its Pupils, 1785–1858* (Philadelphia: J. B. Lippincott, 1858), 129.

35. Reichel, *History of the Rise, Progress, and Present Condition of the Bethlehem Seminary*, 130–31.

36. Reichel, *History of the Rise, Progress, and Present Condition of the Bethlehem Seminary*, 54.

37. The Reverend Vernon Nelson of Bethlehem delivered a paper at the spring 2007 Moravian conference that illuminated a possibility of Anna Rosina's botanical connection with the faculty at the Moravian seminary in Barby, Germany.

38. Myers, *Century of Moravian Sisters*, 152.

39. George Henry Loskiel's *History of the Missions of the United Brethren among the Indians of North America*, trans. Christian Ignatius Latrobe (London: Brethren's Society for the Furtherance of the Gospel among the Heathen, 1794).

40. Moravians frequently held mission conferences whereby official business of that particular mission was addressed. The Salem Moravians had appointed Brother John Gambold to preside over conferences at Springplace. The Salem

congregation further instructed the Gambolds with the following directives: "John Gambold will hold a Mission Conference every two weeks, daily services as well as the usual ones on Sunday, lead the Cherokee children to the Savior (the main responsibility), and supervise all the supplies. Sister Gambold will instruct and educate the Cherokee children and take the children to the services, especially the *Singstunde* (hymn sermon). Sister Dorothea née Schneider Byhan (1803–1812) will take care of the Negress, Pleasant, and the washing; and Brother Gottlieb Byhan will assist Brother Gambold in the services." Correspondence, Communication of the Provincial Helpers' Conference in Salem to the Mission Conference in Springplace, September 1805, MAS.

41. A significant place name, Mountjoy was the home of Margaret Ann Scott Vann Crutchfield (the first Moravian Cherokee convert and former wife of well-known deceased Cherokee James Vann) and her husband, Joseph. The noted Moravian minister Johann Schweishaupt and his wife, Anna Maria Ritterberger, lived in Lititz, the area of Mountjoy. Lititz Diary, MAB, 33–34. The impression that Mountjoy, Pennsylvania, made on Anna Rosina perhaps influenced the naming of the Crutchfield's home place as the same place name, Mountjoy.

42. George Heinrich Loskiel, *Extempore on a Wagon: A Metrical Narrative of a Journey from Bethlehem, Pa., to the Indian Town of Goshen, Ohio, in the Autumn of 1803* (Lancaster PA: S. H. Zahm, 1887), iii, iv, 1, 41.

43. Loskiel, *Extempore on a Wagon*, 41. Goshen, founded in October 1798 by Zeisberger and his followers from Fairfield, Canada, was located about seven miles northeast from Gnadenhütten, on the west bank of the Tuscarawas River in Goshen Township, Tuscarawas County, Ohio. In 1824 the Indians left to join the Indian congregation at New Fairfield, Canada (iii).

44. Loskiel, *Extempore on a Wagon*, 37–39.

45. Rachel Wheeler, "Women and Christian Practice in a Mahican Village," in *Religion and American Culture: A Journal of Interpretation* 13, no. 1 (Summer 2002): 30. Wheeler notes that even converted and friendly Indians lived at eighteenth-century mission sites, but that was not the case at Springplace Mission, where all Cherokees, whether converted or not, did not live on the mission premises. The Gambolds were opposed to such arrangements. "They claimed that congregating in communities would not be suitable for the Cherokees and that even the government (U.S.) would not welcome it, since it is endeavoring to make agriculture the main occupation of the Indians and living separately would afford that opportunity; the government goes to pains to have them live in dispersed localities. . . . . Only few acres are to be found where a tract of good land exists in one place large enough for the needs of a Cherokee farming community with its present husbandry methods, and in part such places already are

occupied. Also those connected to us own from 4 to 19 Negro slaves who can multiply year by year, it must be evident first of all that considerable space would be needed for the dwellings and the maintenance of the Negroes and further that it would be more of a Negro town than an Indian. For example, Brother and Sister Crutchfield [Peggy and Joseph] would have moved closer to Springplace before now, but are unable to do so because of their Negroes; and our closest neighbor, Joseph Vann, whose field borders on Springplace, also has a large number of Negroes, namely more than 70. Now when that fact is added that our Cherokees are tillers of the soil and farmers, some of whom have extensive fields and numerous herds of horses, cattle, pits, and sheep, how could they live together in one place, unless their fields would be several miles away? And where should they keep their numerous herds? To what a lot of clashes and occasions for provocation their living together would lead! In short, they are farmers and in this country farmers cannot live together in a village. If the time should come when this country would be so advanced as to provide constantly for craftsmen and native-born individuals would fill these positions, only then would it be advisable to propose their living together." Hamilton, "Minutes of the Mission Conference Held in Springplace," 37.

46. The Moravians translated the German term *Heide* (heathen) and *Heiden* (heathens) interchangeably as the singular "heathen," so this abridgment mostly uses "heathen," but the German is plural (*Heiden*) in most cases. Zinzendorf's protégé and Moravian bishop of the Northern Province (Bethlehem) August Gottlieb Spangenberg wrote the treatise on Moravian perceptions of the "heathen" as those people who had not entered into a covenant relationship with God and his Son Jesus Christ. He postulated that other peoples, not covenanted like the Israelites, through no fault of their own, lacked knowledge of God's contract and historic perception to share "in this peculiar covenant of grace," so they were generally considered aliens and commonly called "heathen." Spangenberg admonished Moravians in this way: "Do not be terrified by the inhuman wickedness prevailing among the heathen and do not be deceived by appearances, as though the heathen were already good sort of people." August Gottlieb Spangenberg, *An Account of the Manner in Which the Protestant Church of the Unitas Fratrum, or United Brethren, Preach the Gospel and Carry on Their Missions among the Heathen* (Barby, Germany, December 12, 1780), 1, 2, 45–46.

47. Jon F. Sensbach, "Race and the Early Moravian Church: A Comparative Study," *Transactions of the Moravian Historical Society* 31 (2000): 1–11. For the relationship of Moravians and peoples of African descent, see Sensbach, *A Separate Canaan: The Making of an Afro-Moravian World in North Carolina, 1763–1840* (Chapel Hill: University of North Carolina Press, 1998).

48. David Crantz, *The History of Greenland Containing a Description of the Country and Its Inhabitants: and Particularly, a Relation of the Mission, Carried on for Above These Thirty Years by the Unitas Fratrum, at New Herrnhut and Lichtenfels, in that Country*, 2 vols. (London: The Brethren's Society for the Furtherance of the Gospel among the Heathen, 1767), 1:316, 317.

Others were accepted as well. For example, Moravian convert Andrew the Moor, a free African, performed all the duties of membership, including the preparation of a *Lebenslauf* (Memoir or Life's Journey), which was a long-standing custom among Moravians, regardless of race, sex, or class. Autobiographers tended to focus on significant spiritual affairs, but some pointed out aspects of their temporal lives as well. Thorp, *Moravian Community in Colonial North Carolina*, 52–57; and Thorp, "Chattel with a Soul: The Autobiography of a Moravian Slave," *Pennsylvania Magazine of History and Biography* 112 (1988): 433–51. For an in-depth study of the relationship between Moravians and peoples of African descent, see Sensbach, *A Separate Canaan.*

49. Crantz, *History of Greenland*, 1:316, 317.

50. According to Moravians, human worthiness did not mean salvation; salvation, they argued, sprang from the work of the Holy Spirit. David A. Schattschneider, "The Missionary Theologies of Zinzendorf and Spangenberg," *Transactions of the Moravian Historical Society* 22, pt. 3 (1975): 216–19.

51. Joseph Edmund Hutton, *A History of Moravian Missions* (London: Moravian Publishing Office, 1923), 174–76; and Arthur J. Lewis, *Zinzendorf, the Ecumenical Pioneer: A Study in the Moravian Contribution to Christian Unity* (Philadelphia: Westminster Press, 1962), 92.

52. Sensbach, "Interracial Sects: Religion, Race, and Gender among Early North Carolina Moravians," in *The Devil's Lane: Sex and Race in the Early South*, ed. Catherine Clinton and Michele Gillespie (New York: Oxford University Press, 1997), 162.

53. For an in-depth study of Moravians and African Americans, see Sensbach, *Rebecca's Revival: Creating Black Christianity in the Atlantic World* (Cambridge MA: Harvard University Press, 2005); and Sensbach, "Interracial Sects," 154–67.

54. Paul Peucker, "From All Nations: Non-Europeans in the European Moravian Church around 1750" (paper presented at the Moravian Archives Friends' Day, Bethlehem PA, March 13, 2005).

55. See Sensbach, *Rebecca's Revival.*

56. Female student Mary Young of Maryland insulted Sister Maria in unthinkable ways, and it pained her so that her career in teaching came to a sudden halt. Charlotte B. Mortimer, *Bethlehem and Bethlehem School* (New York: Stanford and Delisser, 1858), 135–37.

57. C. B. Mortimer, *Bethlehem and Bethlehem School* (New York: Stanford and Delisser, 1858), 135–37.

58. Bela Baker Edwards, *The Memoir of the Rev. Elias Cornelius*, 2nd ed. (Boston: Perkins, Marvin, and Co., 1834); the quote is on 89. In 1817 the traveling New Englander and Congregationalist minister the Reverend Elias Cornelius recommended that Anna Rosina publish her botanical contributions; Yale professor Benjamin Silliman's scientific journal, the *American Journal of Science*, published her article. A few years earlier, a Lutheran minister and well-known herbal collector, the Reverend Gotthilf Heinrich (Henry) Ernst Mühlenberg of Lancaster, Pennsylvania, had gathered a number of Anna Rosina's Cherokee seeds and had them labeled for his Muhlenberg Herbarium now housed in the Academy of Natural Science of the American Philosophical Society. Mortimer, *Bethlehem and Bethlehem School*, 152–53. For a list of her Springplace plants, see Mrs. Anna Rosina Gambold, "Plants of the Cherokee County: 'A list of plants found in the neighborhood of Connasarga River, (Cherokee Country), where Springplace is situated,' made by Mrs. Gambold, at the request of the Rev. Elias Cornelius," *American Journal of Science* (New York: J. Eastburn and Co., 1818–19), 1:245–51. See Daniel L. McKinley, "Anna Rosina (Kliest) Gambold (1762–1821), Moravian Missionary to the Cherokees, with Special Reference to her Botanical Interests," *Transactions of the Moravian Historical Society* 28 (1994): 59–99.

59. Edwards, *Memoir of the Rev. Elias Cornelius*, 87.

60. The missionaries preferred corn, the hybrid kind, to Indian corn, which they considered coarse and harder to mill.

61. Chickens, sheep, and goats, like pigs and cows, were "new fauna" among the Cherokees, probably accepted by the Cherokees late in the eighteenth century. Gary C. Goodwin, *Cherokees in Transition: A Study of Changing Culture and Environment prior to 1775* (Chicago: University of Chicago Press, 1977), 132.

62. Hamilton, "Minutes of the Mission Conference Held in Springplace," 51; and Schwarze, *History of the Moravian Missions*, 134. German settlers built drying houses to dry fruits before the advent of canning in the mid–nineteenth century. A period German farm with a drying house, bake oven, and other period buildings is Quiet Valley, dating from 1765, located near Stroudsburg, Pennsylvania.

63. Edwards, *Memoir of the Rev. Elias Cornelius*, 87.

64. See the aforementioned article by Mrs. Anna Gambold, "Plants of the Cherokee Country."

65. Edwards, *Memoir of the Rev. Elias Cornelius*, 88.

66. John Gottlieb Ernestus Heckewelder, *Thirty Thousand Miles with John Heckewelder*, ed. Paul A. W. Wallace (Pittsburgh: University of Pittsburgh Press, 1958); and Heckewelder, *Narrative of the Missions of the United Brethren*.

67. Paul A. W. Wallace, "John Heckewelder's Indians and the Fenimore Cooper Tradition," *Proceedings of the American Philosophical Society* 96 (August 1952): 504.

1. Significant Events and Themes

1. A separate *Gemeinhaus* (congregational house) was built in 1819 that replaced the barn for church services.

2. In "Native Voices in a Colonial World," chapter 4 of *Facing East from Indian Country: A Native History of Early American* (Cambridge MA: Harvard University Press, 2001), David Richter develops a very clear Puritan morphology; he explains how Native voice surfaces while Puritan morphology creates concrete roadblocks to discourage conversion. (I am grateful to David Nichols for redirecting my attention to Richter's significant contribution to perceiving ways to read Puritan documents to tease out the Native voice.)

3. In 1817 the American Moravian Church expressed concerns over the invasiveness of the lot and presented a list of grievances about this church practice and others at the 1818 General Synod in Barby, Germany, but to no avail. Joseph Mortimer Levering, *A History of Bethlehem, Pennsylvania, 1741–1892, With Some Account of Its Founders and Their Early Activity* (Bethlehem: Time Publishing Company, 1903), 611–15.

4. The form of the service of Holy Communion stemmed from the earliest days of the *Unitas Fratrum* (Unity of the Brethren) whereby the communicants stood to receive the sacraments, both bread and wine. Adelaide L. Fries, *Customs and Practices of the Moravian Church* (Winston-Salem NC: Board of Christian Education and Evangelism, 1962; reprint, 1973), 31, 32.

5. As Charles Hicks played many roles in the Cherokee Nation during Anna Rosina Gambold's tenure (second principal chief, interpreter, and treasurer), he was absent from many services and Holy Communions, so he sent letters or notes frequently to the Gambolds to let them know the reasons for his absences.

In the translation section (1805–1821) of this edition of the Springplace Diary, the early nineteenth-century missionaries frequently employed the term *Privatunterredung* (private conversation) when promoting spiritual guidance for mission visitors. This term must not be confused with *das Sprechen* (speaking), which was only used for communicants.

6. The date of August 13 was commemorative of the founding of the Renewed Moravian Church on August 13, 1727.

7. Margaret Scott Vann (c. 1781–1820), daughter of Walter Scott and Sarah Hicks Scott Brown, married James Vann and lived at Diamond Hill; she was a distant relative of Chiconehla (Nancy Ward). After Vann's death, she married Joseph Crutchfield and moved to Mountjoy, on the west side of the Conasauga River, and became a Moravian on August 13, 1810.

Moravians gave their Indian converts names of famous Christians or saints. In the case of Margaret Scott Vann, the name Margaret designated the martyr during the Diocletian persecutions; the Moravians added Ann, Jesus' grandmother's name. Likewise, Charles was the anglicized version of Charlemagne, first emperor of the Holy Roman Empire. The Moravians added Renatus, or Rebirth, for his middle name, which was the name of Zinzendorf's son, Christian Renatus.

8. Many of the children were related to James Vann, his multiple wives, and Sarah Hicks Scott Brown's offspring from her first husband, Walter Scott, and second husband, Robert Brown. Other baptisms followed between 1819 and 1822: William Abraham Hicks and his wife, Sarah Bethniah Foreman Hicks (Sally); Susanna Ridge (wife of Major Ridge); Delilah Amelia McNair; Lydia Halfbreed (Zaujuka) and her mother, Catherina (Catherine Gann); Nancy Vann Talley (Anna Dorothea); Betsy Lassley; Susanna, wife of Watie; Nancy Adair; Anna Felicitas (Nancy Hicks) and her mother, Ajosta; Christina Maria (Mother Vann), and Clement Vann. Schwarze, *History of the Moravian Missions*, 142–72.

9. Anniversary of the founding of the Renewed Moravian Church on the estate of Count Nicholas Ludwig von Zinzendorf at Herrnhut (Saxony), Germany, on August 13, 1727.

10. *Erstling*. Or first fruits (converts).

11. Betsy Scott.

12. Sarah Hicks Scott Brown.

13. English in the German manuscript.

14. Among the Cherokees, it was the custom to retain the maiden name on the father's side, because the missionaries contended that "Indians changed husbands frequently." Hence, she kept the name Scott. Cherokee women also kept their given names, such as Jenny, Nancy, and Peggy. The missionaries recorded that they respected this Indian custom. Correspondence, John and Anna Rosina Gambold to Carl Gotthold Reichel, September 15, 1810, MAS.

15. Isabel and Charlotte Brown were half-sisters of Peggy.

16. Charles [Renatus] Hicks (1767–1827), son of white trader Nathan Hicks and a half-Cherokee woman whose lineage is unknown but was probably a sister of Gunrod; born at Tomaatly on the Hiwassee River; fluent in English; married Nancy Broom Hicks. He served as interpreter for Indian agent Meigs, a position that ended when he opposed Doublehead's 1807 secret plan to sell Cherokee land. He became treasurer of the Cherokee Nation in 1813 and second principal chief next to Principal Chief Pathkiller in 1817, and he remained in that position until assuming the title of principal chief in 1827. He died shortly thereafter. A patron of the Moravians, he joined the Moravian Church in 1813 and received the baptismal name Charles Renatus. Hicks. See "The Memoir of Charles Renatus

Hicks (*Lebenslauf*)," *The United Brethren Missionary Intelligencer* 2 (First Quarter 1827), MAS; and Rowena McClinton Ruff, "Notable Persons in Cherokee History: Charles Hicks," *Journal of Cherokee Studies* 17 (1996): 16–27.

17. English word in the German manuscript.

18. Robert Brown, of Chickamauga, Tennessee, and father of James, John, Jenny, Ann, and Moravian students Charlotte and Isabel, and stepfather of Peggy Scott Vann Crutchfield. His second wife was Sarah Hicks Scott.

19. Captain David McNair, son of Scots trader David McNair; married Delilah Amelia Vann, a daughter of James Vann and Betsy Scott. He kept a boat stand at the southern end of the portage on the Conasauga River, called Owakoi, just inside the Tennessee line. He became a "Cherokee countryman," administrator of Vann's estate, and loyal friend of the Moravians. He attained the rank of captain in the Creek War of 1813–14. He was superintendent for elections to the 1827 Constitutional Convention from the Amohee District. When Georgia citizens forced the missionaries out of Springplace on January 1, 1833, they fled to McNair's on the Georgia-Tennessee border, where they operated a small mission school on his premises until 1836. Under the Treaty of New Echota, his improvements were valued at over twelve thousand dollars. He and Delilah had six children. Gary Moulton, ed., *The Papers of Chief John Ross* (Norman: University of Oklahoma Press, 1985), 2:738; Schwarze, *History of the Moravian Missions*, 138; Don L. Shadburn, "Cherokee Statesmen: The John Rogers Family of Chattahoochee," *Chronicles of Oklahoma* 50 (Spring 1972): 12–40.

20. The terms Brethren, Brother, and Sister were terms only given to Moravian communicants.

21. Named after the only son of Zinzendorf, Christian Renatus (Rebirth), who was also deceased.

22. Charles Hicks was afflicted with a disease called the "king's evil," or scrofula americana, a form of tuberculosis that consisted of tumors in various glands of the body. It was the most common kind associated with Cherokees like Hicks and Moravian student John Ridge, son of Major and Susanna (Wicked) Ridge. See Robert Hooper, *Lexicon Medicum; or Medical Dictionary*, 13th ed. (New York: Harper and Brothers, 1843), 1:274–75.

23. Nancy Broom Hicks, who was baptized a Moravian in July of 1821 and received the name Ann Felicitas, was named for Anna Rosina's mother Anna Felicitas née Schuster Kliest (1729–1765), born in Würzberg, Germany. See Schwarze's *History of the Moravian Missions*, 65–66; and *Lebensläufe* folder, MAS.

24. Joseph Crutchfield was the husband of Peggy Scott Vann, the former widow of James Vann. They married in 1812 and he became a Moravian in September of 1814.

25. Alice Shorey, the daughter of Chief William Shorey and an unknown mother, and the niece of John and Anne Shorey McDonald, was a Moravian student who entered the mission school on July 23, 1809.

26. English in the German manuscript.

27. Nancy Ridge (c. 1798), daughter of The Ridge (later Major Ridge) and Susanna Wickett (Wicked) of Oothcaloga. She entered the mission school June 15, 1810 and left August 21, 1812. She married William Ritchie in 1818 and died in childbirth, September 14, 1819.

28. Samuel Talley, Vann's overseer.

29. Or James Brown, son of Robert Brown of Chickamauga and stepbrother of Peggy Scott Vann Crutchfield.

30. The disputed will of James Vann bequeathed his son Joseph Vann the bulk of the Vann estate until the National Council ruled that his wife Peggy was entitled to some land and slaves. Rennard Strickland, *Fire and the Spirits: Cherokee Law from Clan to Court* (Norman: University of Oklahoma Press, 1975), 97–99.

31. English in the German manuscript.

32. Gottlieb and Dorothea Byhan, missionaries to the Cherokees from 1801 to 1812 and again from 1827 to 1832.

33. *Treaties between the United States of America and the Cherokee Nation, from 1785* (Tahlequah, Cherokee Nation: National Printing Office, 1870), 24–59.

34. William S. Lovely, assistant Indian agent to Colonel Meigs from 1801 until 1812, when he was assigned to the Arkansas Cherokees.

35. Actually, the next fall of 1807.

36. Chuleoa (Chu,li,oa or Chu,le,o,ah or Chul,lI,o), also known as Gentleman Tom. Upper Town leader; among the initial group of Cherokees who negotiated with Moravians for a mission school; stipulated that Moravians teach English, not German; grandson Tommy Acaraca or Whirlwind entered the mission school in 1804.

37. Kotoquaski (John McIntosh, Gotoquasky, or Quotaquskey) of Hiwassee; married Jennie Walker, descendant of Ghigau (Nancy Ward); son Fox was a student at the Blackburn school at Hiwassee; ardent opponent of removal.

38. William Abraham (b. 1769) Hicks, brother of Charles and sister of Sarah Hicks Scott Brown; father was Nathan and mother was probably the sister of Gunrod. He had several marriages: Zaujuka Halfbreed (Lydia) and Sarah (Bethniah) Foreman. In 1819 William Hicks enrolled another son, Eli, into the mission school. He became a Moravian convert with the name William Abraham. His son by Zaujuka was George; he had thirteen children by Sarah (Bethniah) Foreman: Eli, Jay, Ruth, William, Carrington, Margaret, Ella, Abijah, Anna, Charles, John, Sarah, and Nannie.

39. Tommy Acaraca or Whirlwind (Ak,a,no,ock or Aiaruea) (born c. 1794), age ten; named Tommy or Tom by the missionaries because they could not pronounce his Cherokee name; he entered the mission school October 8, 1804; left August 24, 1809. Son or grandson of Chuleoa or Gentleman Tom of Hightower; stepson of Nancy Hughes; mother deceased.

40. Samuel Hall, government blacksmith. A neighbor of the Moravians, he sometimes supplied and sold them necessities such as pigs. He later moved to the Hiwassee Garrison.

41. James Vann's white relative and overseer of his Diamond Hill plantation.

42. Alexander Saunders (Sanders), one of eight children by a Cherokee mother, Susannah, and Mitchell Saunders, was a Revolutionary War deserter from New Hampshire who moved to the Cherokee Nation and became a Cherokee countryman, a white whose marriage gave him Cherokee citizenship status. A staunch nationalist, Saunders in 1807 was one of Doublehead's executioners.

43. Major Ridge (c. 1771–1839), or "The Ridge," which means "the man who walks on the mountaintop." His Cherokee name, Nun-na-dihi, or Pathkiller, means "he who slays the enemy in the path"; born on the north bank of the Hiwassee River above present-day Columbus, Polk County Tennessee; married Susanna Catherine Wickett (Wicked); attained rank of major in the Creek War of 1813–14; father of John, Nancy, Watty (Walter), and Sarah.

44. Charles McDonald was possibly the son of Scots trader, David McDonald, who married a Cherokee; one of his Cherokee wives was Tsowaeyakee of Saliquoi (Salacoa).

45. Johnston (Johnson) McDonald (c. 1797–1820), son of Charles McDonald and Tsowaeyakee of Saliquoi (Salacoa), lived at the confluence of the Salacoa Creek and the Oostanaula River; entered the mission school August 16, 1806, at age nine; left August 3, 1811. He was a diligent student and a distant relative of Vann's; he stayed at Vann's along with Robert and Moses Parris; after Vann died, the missionaries agreed to let Johnston stay with them. The McDonalds' grandson Moses entered the school in 1808.

46. Chiquaki, of Hightower, was the grandfather of Moravian student John Gutseyedi.

47. These are diarist's translations.

48. Carsten Petersen (1776–1857), Moravian missionary to the Creeks from 1807 to 1813.

49. Mother Vann's sister.

50. Margaret Ann Scott Vann Crutchfield.

51. Polly Vann, of Hightower; daughter of Chief Terrapin.

52. Chief Bark, of Hightower; great uncle or grandfather of Moravian student George Vann.

53. The Moravian missionaries to the Creeks, Carsten Petersen and Timothy Holland (b. 1793). They were on one of their frequent visits to Springplace Mission.

54. Dawzizi, son of The Tyger and Oodeisaski (Smith) of Big Spring, entered the mission school September 20, 1810, at age twelve; left August 18, 1817.

55. Since the end of the Creek War, Indian agent Meigs was so preoccupied with problems associated with General Andrew Jackson's refusal to pay the six hundred Cherokee warriors for their services that he delayed the annuity meeting until the fall of 1815 to reimburse the Cherokees for land cessions through the promised annuities already overdue for 1813, 1814, and 1815.

56. Hiwassee Agency.

57. Timothy Meigs died of a bilious fever.

58. To counteract unlawful intruders into their nation, a revitalized National Committee in 1817 continued to limit Cherokee citizenship and residency in the nation. However, blacksmiths, schoolteachers, and missionaries could remain. Hamilton, "Minutes of the Mission Conference," 36; and McLoughlin, *Cherokee Renascence*, 224–27.

59. Since 1811 the National Committee had control over the National Treasury and annuities, but because the National Committee did not meet regularly, Meigs assisted with the administration of the annuity. Meigs and his son Timothy had used annuity payments to settle private claims owed to traders by individual Cherokees. He had charged annuity payments against the disbursement of corn, and he feared that if he continued to charge any more payments of any kind, including white claims against the Cherokees, it would anger the National Committee. In 1817, because of annuity mismanagement, the Cherokee National Treasury took over the sole supervision of annuity payments. McLoughlin, *Cherokee Renascence*, 223–24.

60. Ridge to President Monroe, March 8, 1821, Ayer Collection, Box 761, Newberry Library, Chicago.

61. McLoughlin, "Cherokee Anomie, 1768–1809," chapter 1 of *Cherokee Ghost Dance*, 9–10.

62. McLoughlin, *Cherokee Ghost Dance*, quote on p. 10; and Richard Peters, *The Case of the Cherokee Nation against the State of Georgia* (Philadelphia, 1831), 253.

63. Mabel Haller, *Early Moravian Education in Pennsylvania* (Nazareth PA: Moravian Historical Society, 1953), 234–35.

64. Hamilton, "Minutes of the Mission Conference Held at Springplace," 39.

65. David Hogan, "The Market Revolution and Disciplinary Power: Joseph Lancaster and the Psychology of Early Classroom System," *History of Education Quarterly* 29, no. 3 (Fall 1989): 381–417. Refer also to Dell Upton's "Lancasterian Schools, Republican Citizenship, and the Spatial Imagination in Early Nineteenth-Century America," in *Journal of the Society of Architectural Historians* 55, no. 3 (September 1996): 238–53.

66. Englishman Joseph Lancaster formulated a mass public education system whereby older students monitored and instructed younger ones. Ronald Rayman, "Joseph Lancaster's Monitorial System of Instruction and American Indian Education, 1815–1838," *History of Education Quarterly* 21 (Winter 1981): 395–410.

67. Johnny Gutseyedi or Gutseysdi (c. 1795), son of Dunawee and Tsikisk; grandson of Chiquaki of Hightower and Enoli (Black Fox); entered the mission school August 18, 1805, at age ten; left April 30, 1811.

68. Dick Dyeentohee (c. 1795), son of Dick and Goadi of Chickamauga; grandson of The Flea; entered the mission school July 28, 1807, at age twelve; left December 26, 1809.

69. Dick's family lived in Chickamauga, near present-day Chattanooga, Tennessee.

70. Alice (Elsy or Eley) Shorey (b. June 15, 1798), daughter of the late Chief William Shorey; mother unknown; entered the mission school July 23, 1809, at age eleven; left April 17, 1811. She married Nathan Wolf Hicks on April 12, 1812.

71. According to Anna Rosina's article "A list of plants . . . in Cherokee Country" in the *American Journal of Science*, 250, a tea to relieve fever is made from the bark of the root of *Liriodendrum tulipifera*.

72. Dick of Chickamauga.

73. John Ridge (c. 1800), son of The Ridge (later Major Ridge) and Susanna Wickett (Wicked) of Oothcaloga; age ten; entered the mission school November 12, 1810; departed April 12, 1815.

74. Daughter of Robert and Sarah Hicks Scott Brown of Lookout Mountain Town; age eight; entered the mission school September 4, 1809; departed December 7, 1812.

75. Buck Ooaty (Watie) (Galagina or Kiakeena), later Elias Boudinot (c. 1804–1839), the son of David Watie (Ooaty) and Susanna Reece of Oothcaloga. His name represents a male deer, which is the reason he is given the name Buck Ooaty (Watie) at Springplace, where he attended from 1810 to 1815, and again from 1816 to 1818. He was sent to Cornwall in 1818 and stayed until 1822; on his first trip east in 1818 Buck met the longtime president of the American Bible Society in Burlington, New Jersey, and Elias Boudinot was so pleased to meet him that he asked Buck to adopt his name.

76. Susanna Wickett (Wicked). Her Indian name was probably Shoya; mother of John, Nancy, Watty (Walter), and Sarah Ridge. She was described as a "handsome and sensible girl." She and The Ridge married in the early 1790s.

77. *Pfingstblumen.* Honeysuckle flower or rush was indigenous to the Cherokees; it grew up to four thousand feet altitude in spruce-fir areas. The term used here literally meant Pentecost flowers. Goodwin, *Cherokees in Transition*, 160.

78. Moravian slave of Springplace Mission; she arrived with the Gambolds October 20, 1805.

79. Turkey Cock and Dully are slaves belonging to the nearby Vann plantation.

80. Sons of George Parris of Oothcaloga; mothers of both sons are sisters; age of Moses is age twelve; Robert is age eleven; they entered Springplace July 29, 1806; both left February 23, 1807. Exact dates of students' departures may vary among the diarist's recordings, the Catalog of Scholars (Moravian Archives Bethlehem), and correspondence from Springplace to Salem.

81. Gentleman Tom or Chuleoa took Tommy home for the Green Corn Dance held at Oostanaula. George Vann behaved better when Tommy was absent. When Tommy returned to the mission, he arrived with his "shirt cut off at the waist." Correspondence, John Gambold to Carl Gotthold Reichel, September 28, 1806, MAS.

82. Also known as the Ripe Green Corn Feast. See Ruth Y. Wetmore's "The Green Corn Ceremony of the Eastern Cherokees" in *Journal of Cherokee Studies* 8 (Spring 1983): 46–56. See chapter 2, this volume, for more information about the Green Corn Feast.

83. Benjamin Hawkins, Indian agent to the Creeks and overall agent appointed to oversee the general conduct of the "Four Nations": Cherokees, Creeks, Choctaws, and Chickasaws.

84. The Moravian missionaries to the Creeks, Carsten Petersen and Timothy Holland.

85. George Vann, of Hightower or Etowah, was the son of John Vann and Polly, daughter of Chief Terrapin.

86. Suakie of Broomtown, a respected Cherokee of the National Council.

87. Nine-year-old Tawoadi, Tawoody, Tawoady, or Great Hawk (*Großer Gaunersich*).

88. Anne Shorey.

89. Long-time resident in Cherokee Nation, king's agent, and Scots trader, John McDonald, of Chickamauga Creek in present-day Chattanooga, Tennessee, was educated in Scotland. He came to live among the Cherokees, and in 1768, he married Anne Shorey, a sister of Chief William Shorey. John and Anne had had two children, Mollie and George (indicated from missionary records).

90. John and Betsy Lowery, the latter the niece of Anne McDonald.

91. John Ross (1790–1866) was a Cherokee leader who served his nation for more than fifty years (principal chief 1828 to 1866); he was instrumental in the centralization of Cherokee government through the 1827 Cherokee Constitution; he vehemently opposed removal and used the court system and congressional petitions to avert displacement; he rebuilt his nation in Indian Territory, only to face desecration during the Civil War, which also factionalized his people into two camps, antislavery and proslavery. When he died in 1866, the Cherokee Nation had just begun to restore itself from devastation, and it soon obtained the strong legacy Ross had inspired. See Gary Moulton, "John Ross," in *Encyclopedia of North American Indians*, ed. Frederick Hoxie (Boston: Houghton Mifflin, 1996), 559–61.

92. Jack Gonstadi (c. 1809), the son of Jim Foster and Qualiyuga, entered the mission school on April 5, 1814, at age five; left February 10, 1819. After his sojourn at Springplace, he joined the Baptist church and became an interpreter for Evan Jones. He married Lucinda Foreman and their son James, or Gahuska, was born in 1843.

93. Nicholas Ludwig Zinzendorf, founder of the Renewed Moravian Church, with scholar Samuel Lieberkuehn, a Moravian missionary in Amsterdam, translated and blended all four gospels into one gospel story.

94. David Watie's wife, Susanna, wanted their son Buck home because their twelve-year-old daughter had died at Springplace. (Dawnee died of severe vomiting on September 27, 1812.)

95. Iskittihi or Fivekiller (Iskytihy, Iskitihy, or Iskittichee) (c. 1793), twelve-year-old son of The Mire and stepson of The Mouse of Rabbit Trap; mother unknown; entered the mission school February 1, 1805. The missionaries recorded that the boy's clothes had to come from the annuity, which granted each child one coat and one blanket. After Iskittihi's departure, the missionaries did not want him to return under any circumstances. Correspondence, John Gambold to Carl Gotthold Reichel, February 5, 1806, MAS. In 1817 the missionaries learned that Iskittihi was shot and killed by accident.

96. Suakee of Spring Place, a town near Springplace Mission; not to be confused with Suakie of Broomtown.

97. September 7th signaled the immovable choir festival for the Married Choir Covenant Day; the lovefeast, an ancient celebration of *Agape*, was a social gathering open to non-Moravians as well. While the Moravians sang hymns, they passed around buns or simple food and coffee.

98. Calhgio.

99. The missionaries noted that Tlaneneh did not inherit "Indian laziness."

Correspondence, John and Anna Rosina Gambold to Christian Lewis Reichel, October 2, 1809, MAS.

100. Jack Still was a relative of Peggy Crutchfield's; in 1836, a valuing agent recorded that Still lived in Cherokee County and owned three slaves; his children are listed as Green, Jim, and Cook Still. He married Aelia. He lived in Tennessee earlier.

101. The community of Pine Log is located in present-day northeast Bartow County (Georgia) in the vicinity of Hightower.

102. Pleasant.

103. Perhaps Patience, who lost both feet to frostbite when she was marched from Charleston to the Vann plantation, Diamond Hill, in the winter of 1806.

104. Mary Vann (b. 1795), daughter of James and Ann Vann of Diamond Hill, near Springplace Mission; entered the mission school at age ten and left in 1807; she married Fox Taylor. The diarist refers to Margaret Ann Scott Vann, though Mary is the daughter of one of James Vann's other wives.

105. Robin (c. 1801), son of James Vann or Water Hunter and Dawnee (below Oostanaula); entered the mission school November 20, 1815, at age fourteen; dismissed July 1817 for bad behavior.

106. George; father unknown. George entered the mission school June 20, 1818.

107. Woki or Peggy. She died in the spring of 1815.

108. Stand Watie or Ooaty.

109. English in the German manuscript.

110. The missionaries thought she ate a poisonous plant, the flower of the thorn apple or stinkweed (*Datura stramonium*). For her burial they selected a hill about three hundred feet southwest of the mission, so that from their yard they could see the gravesite.

111. Mother Vann.

112. Peggy or Woki.

113. McLoughlin, "Cherokee Anomie, 1768–1809" in *Cherokee Ghost Dance*, 3–39.

114. For in depth studies of alcohol among the Indians, see Peter C. Mancall, "Costs," chapter 4 of *Deadly Medicine: Indians and Alcohol in Early America* (Ithaca NY: Cornell University Press, 1995), 85–100; W. J. Rorabaugh, *The Alcoholic Republic: An American Tradition* (New York: Oxford University Press, 1979), 156, 159, 178, 246; and Robin Room, "Alcohol and Ethnography: A Case of Problem Deflation," *Current Anthropology* 5 (April 1984): 175. For works pertaining to alcohol and Cherokees, see Izumi Ishii, *Bad Fruit of the Civilized Tree: Alcohol and Sovereignty of the Cherokee Nation* (Lincoln: University of Nebraska Press, 2008).

115. Young Wolf, son of Onai and The Gunrod. The Young Wolf had the following siblings: The Hair (Hare), The Rattling Gourd, The Crawler, who died as a result of the Creek War, and sister Quatie; he married Jane (Jennie) Taylor, and three of their children—Anna, Peggy, and Dennis—attended Springplace; died of consumption in 1814 and left a will.

116. Peggy Wolf, daughter of The Young Wolf and Jane or Jennie (Taylor) Wolf.

117. David Watie.

118. Anna Rosina mentioned on occasion that Indians can speak English when they are drinking.

119. William Hicks, the brother of Charles, was visiting.

120. Son of the Moravians' slave, Pleasant.

121. Cat or Waesa (Wasa). The Cat was a popular name.

122. Hamilton, "Minutes of the Mission Conference Held in Springplace," 51; and Schwarze, *History of the Moravian Missions*, 134.

123. Helen Hornbeck Tanner, "The Land and Water Communication Systems of the Southeastern Indians," in *Powhatan's Mantle: Indians in the Colonial Southeast*, ed. Peter H. Wood, Gregory A. Waselkov, and M. Thomas Hatley (Lincoln: University of Nebraska Press, 1989), 6–20.

124. Anna, wife of Josiah Vann, distant relative of James Vann.

125. Worli, mother of James Vann.

126. Thomas Busby, millwright and carpenter by trade.

127. Margaret (née Scott) Vann, wife of James Vann, also known as Peggy.

128. Colonel Return Jonathan Meigs, Revolutionary War hero, Indian agent to the Cherokees, 1801–23.

129. Ghigau (Ghi,ga,u). "Beloved 'War' Woman" Nancy Ward. She married Kingfisher and Bryan Ward. Cherokee genealogists Jack Baker, Jerry Clark, and David Hampton believe that most likely Chiconehla was Nancy Ward.

130. Betsy, Nancy Ward's daughter by Bryan Ward. (Note is corrected from vol. 1 of *Moravian Springplace Mission to the Cherokees*.) Emmet Starr, *History of the Cherokee Indians and Their Legends and Folklore* (1921; reprint, Tulsa: Oklahoma Yesterday Publications, 1993), 350.

131. This statement only reiterated what the missionaries observed earlier, which was that "the Indians were unconcerned with what awaited them in life beyond life on earth." Correspondence, Gottlieb Byhan to Christian Lewis Benzien, October 30, 1806, MAS.

132. See Carl F. Klinck and James J. Talman, eds., *The Journal of Major John Norton*, 1816 (Toronto: Champlain Society, 1970). Norton's sojourn among the Cherokees gave rise to linguistic connections between Iroquois and Cherokee

languages. For another approach to the same topic, see Duane H. King, "Who Really Discovered the Cherokee-Iroquois Linguistic Relationship," *Journal of Cherokee Studies* 2, no. 4 (Fall 1977): 401–4.

133. French and Indian War or Seven Years' War.

134. In the aftermath of the American Revolutionary War, Chickamauga warrior Dragging Canoe and other warriors fought the settlers encroaching on their lands. See Penelope Johnson Allen, "Manuscript of the History of the Cherokee Indians, Particularly the Chickamauga Group," 1935, McClung Collection, East Tennessee Historical Society, Knoxville TN.

135. Wampum was a widely used eastern seacoast shell; beads cut from wampum were sewn into belts signifying alliances or used as decorative pieces.

136. Benjamin Henry Latrobe (1764–1820). Noted Moravian architect for the White House in Washington. See chapters 13, 14, and 18 in Talbot Hamlin Faulkner's *Benjamin Henry Latrobe* (New York: Oxford University Press, 1955).

137. Fairfield was the Moravian mission in Canada.

138. The best-known Moravian missionary, David Zeisberger (1721–1808), whose missionary service spanned sixty-two years, ministered mainly to the Delaware but to the Iroquois very briefly. Within those six decades, he encountered hostilities, multiple tribal alliances, and constant displacements; his very survival depended on his moving from one missionary post to another. The crucial years 1772 to 1782 brought Zeisberger into explosive encounters with settlers while he protected Indian converts in Ohio and Pennsylvania missions at Friedenstadt, Schönbrunn, and Gnadenhütten. His Indian missions provoked hostilities with British, French, Americans, and their Indians allies. Consequently the Moravian stance on nonviolence was compromised over and over again. Such was the case with the 1782 Gnadenhütten massacre, whereby American soldiers pillaged, burned, and killed approximately one hundred Christian Indians (Delaware). Zeisberger remained in the Ohio backcountry on the Muskingum River until American-British hostilities had ceased. By the 1790s he established several more missions in the Ohio backcountry but he remained at the Goshen mission on the Tuscawaras (Muskingum) River until his death in 1808. Zeisberger's doughty but diplomatic persona caused some to call him a benevolent despot because he imposed very strict pious laws on Christian Indians. He insisted on belief in one God; respect for elders, including parents; examination by and absolute obedience to teachers; rest on Sundays; exclusion of thieves, murderers, whoremongers, adulterers, or drunkards; prohibition of dances, sacrifices, "heathenish" festivals or games; monogamy; abstinence from intoxicating liquors; permission from the ministers or stewards before going hunting; and the prohibition of war and buying anything taken from warriors in war. His contributions to Indian-German culture included

developing Delaware-German and Onondago-German lexicons. For definitive studies of Zeisberger, see Earl P. Olmstead, *Blackcoats among the Delawares: David Zeisberger on the Ohio Frontier* (Kent OH: Kent State University Press, 1991); David de Schweinitz, *The Life and Times of David Zeisberger, the Western Pioneer and Apostle of the Indians* (Philadelphia: J. B. Lippincott, 1870; reprint, New York: Arno Press, 1971), 378–79; Carola Wessel, "Connecting Congregations: The Net of Communication among the Moravians as Exemplified by the Interaction between Pennsylvania, the Upper Ohio, and Germany (1772–1774)," in *The Distinctiveness of Moravian Culture: Essays and Documents in Moravian History in Honor of Vernon H. Nelson on his Seventieth Birthday*, ed. Craig D. Atwood and Peter Vogt (Nazareth PA: Moravian Historical Society), 153–72; and Wessel and Hermann Wellenreuter, eds., *The Moravian Mission Diaries of David Zeisberger* (University Park PA: Pennsylvania State University Press, 2005).

139. *Handel und Wandel.* (Other translations are "business transactions" and "thrive and strive.") For information on the dramatic changes to the Cherokee economy that came with the use of money, see James L. Douthat, "Colonel Return Jonathan Meigs' Day Book," no. 2 (Signal Mountain TN: Institute for Historical Research, n.d.); and Records of the Cherokee Indian Agency in Tennessee, 1801–1835, Bureau of Indian Affairs, Record Group 75, M208, microfilm rolls 1–9, National Archives, Washington DC.

140. When asked to explain the Cherokee language, McDonald pointed out that he would say a few words phonetically for the missionaries to write down, but that no Indian would understand them. He gave examples the missionaries transposed from Cherokee sounds to German phonics: Father, *O, toa'da* (daddy or floor board); Word, *Can,no'ca* (to speak); Sin or Evil, *Wie,o'ie* (really bad); Life, *Kin ha'*; Blood, *Gie'ga*; the pronoun I (or *ich* in German), no equivalent (no pronoun in Cherokee); Obedience, Go,hi,jus,'ha (he obeys); Truth, *Es,to,hi,ju*; Body, *I,di,cel,le*; Hope, *On,tut,ga'go*; I hope, *ha*; Satan or the Devil, *Shie'na*; Heaven, *Cul le'li,ti* (great height, the highest floor in a house; others say *Garreridi*, or garret, presumably); Happiness, *O,si'u,ey, geindan,'ta*; Death, *Ey,a,hu,ha*, or *Eyahuhi* (he is dead); Sufferings, *O,giel,his,u* (he is suffering); Disobedience, *In,cla,go,hi,jus'* or *ka* (he does not obey); Knowledge, *Ou,tan,te* (he has sense); House, *Gol,zot'a*; Love, Kehn, ke,ju,ha (I love you). Charles Hicks told the missionaries that the language had taken on a different form in the last one hundred years. Correspondence, Anna Rosina Gambold to Carl Gotthold Reichel, December 30, 1809, MAS.

141. Relative of neighbor Peggy Vann.

142. Sam Houston, of Tennessee, also known as The Raven. Later governor of Tennessee and Texas.

143. Catholic abbot Correa de Serra.

144. Francis W. Gilmer.

145. James Monroe (1758–1831). He, his wife, Elizabeth Kortright (1763–1830), the daughter of a New York merchant, and his son, James, visited Vann's plantation, May 24, 1819. Harold D. Moser, ed., *The Papers of Andrew Jackson*, vol. 4: *1816–1820* (Knoxville: University of Tennessee Press, 1994), 30.

146. The Brainerd Mission, near present-day Chattanooga, Tennessee, was named for New England missionary David Brainerd. For a definitive history of the Brainerd Mission, see William G. McLoughlin, *Cherokees and Missionaries, 1789–1839* (New Haven CT: Yale University Press, 1984); Joyce B. Phillips and Paul Gary Phillips, eds., *The Brainerd Journal: A Mission to the Cherokees, 1817–1823* (Lincoln: University of Nebraska Press, 1998); and Walker, *Torchlights to the Cherokees.*

147. McLoughlin, *Cherokees and Missionaries*, 94–97. See also McLoughlin's "New Angles of Vision on the Cherokee Ghost Movement of 1811–1812," *American Indian Quarterly* 5: (1979): 317–37.

148. Two travelers from Tennessee had been along the Mississippi River and had seen a whole section of the little city New Madrid, near the confluence of the Ohio and Mississippi rivers, go under. Correspondence, John Gambold to Johannes Herbst, January 18, 1812, MAS.

149. Earlier in the year Hicks wrote the following: "The Ways and order of the Universe are unsearchable and may we adore the God of Mercies for preserving us from Day to Day and may He make us better for the future to come." Correspondence, John Gambold to Johannes Herbst, January 18, 1812, MAS.

150. Later called Crowing Rooster. Shoeboot was a captain of one of the Cherokee companies, and he met Jackson in route to the Battle of Horseshoe Bend. Jackson asked him to make a speech. Shoeboot replied, "Me crow like a cock." As he spoke to Jackson, he said next, "No chicken heart in me." Then clapping one hand on his back, and the other on the back of his head, "No shoot him back," Shoeboot added proudly. He changed his hands to his forehead, then to his heart, and said, "But shoot him here." As Bonaparte said, Shoeboot had covered himself in glory and also concealed his wounds; he disappeared and was nowhere to be found. But he reappeared out of nowhere crying, "Cock a Doodle Do." John Howard Payne Papers, 1:33–34, Ayer Collection, Newberry Library, Chicago. For an in-depth study of Shoeboot, see Adriane Strenk, "Tradition and Transformation: Shoe Boots and the Creation of a Cherokee Culture" (University of Kentucky, master's thesis, 1993), 63. Consult also Tiya Alicia Miles, *Ties that Bind: The Story of an Afro-Cherokee Family in Slavery and Freedom* (Berkeley: University of California Press, 2005).

151. Tugalo, Cherokee Beloved Town, was destroyed in the 1700s; located on the upper Savannah River in western South Carolina. *American State Papers: Indian Affairs*, 2 vols., *Documents, Legislative and Executive of the Congress of the United States*, ed. by Walter Lowie, Walter S. Franklin, and Matthew St. Clair Clark (Washington DC: Gales and Seaton, 1832, 1834), 1:327.

152. Perhaps the bark from the sassafras tree was plentiful in the woods and fields and was native to the Cherokees' habitat. Goodwin, *Cherokees in Transition*, 164.

153. See McLoughlin, *Cherokees and Missionaries*, 96, for a similar translation by the late Elizabeth Marx.

154. John Gambold recorded that Indian prophets predicted a deathlike darkness would surround the earth, and when light appeared again, white people would disappear. So Cherokees should put aside what they have received from the whites. Gambold would like to go to the Council to talk about the "real Light," because "even the lies of the Shawnee prophets [Tecumseh] are circulated this far!" Correspondence, John Gambold to Simon Peter, March 21, 1812, MAS.

155. At this Council Gambold met the oldest and most respected chiefs, persons he had never before met. John and Anna Rosina Gambold to Simon Peter, May 11, 1812, MAS. Furthermore, the missionaries noted that repeated requests by the United States for the Cherokees to relinquish their lands caused considerable consternation among their chiefs. They noted that prudent chiefs stood firm. Some viewed the promise of "civilization" as a reason to stay. But others wished to stay if they could live by hunting. John Gambold to Simon Peter, September 22, 1812, MAS.

156. Sour Mush, Sower Mush or Ogosatah (Sows Much); relative of the Watie family; a Cherokee leader who was one of the first to accept the Moravians into Cherokee country; along with Chuleoa asked the Moravians in 1803 to establish a school as soon as possible so that Cherokee children could be educated.

157. English in the German manuscript.

158. See a similar translation by the late Elizabeth Marx in McLoughlin's *Cherokees and Missionaries*, 98.

159. Malone, *Cherokees of the Old South*, 71–73; Wilkins, *Cherokee Tragedy*, 63, 73, 75, 79–80; and Cherokee Delegation to Washington, Address, December 1815, Records of the Cherokee Indian Agency in Tennessee, Record Group 75, M208, reel 6, National Archives.

160. Wilkins, *Cherokee Tragedy*, 80; and Colonel Meigs to the Secretary of War, May 5, 1814, roll 10, and "Claims by Cherokees for losses due to spoliation of U.S. troops during the Creek War," Records of the Office of Indian Affairs, Record Group 75, National Archives.

161. For a discussion of the Cherokees' involvement in the Creek War of 1813–14, "The Creek War," chapter 3 of Wilkins's *Cherokee Tragedy*, 52–80. For a discussion of the Creeks' involvement, see Michael D. Green, *The Politics of Indian Removal: Creek Government and Society in Crisis* (Lincoln: University of Nebraska Press, 1982); Joel W. Martin, *Sacred Revolt: The Muskogees' Struggle for a New World* (Boston: Beacon Press, 1991); and Claudio Saunt, *A New Order of Things: Property, Power, and the Transformation of the Creek Indians, 1733–1816* (Cambridge: Cambridge University Press, 2000).

162. Earlier the Red Sticks had encountered fierce fighting at Brunt Corn Creek and Holy Ground. Frank Lawrence Owsley, *Struggle for Gulf Border Lands: The Creek War and the Battle of New Orleans, 1812–1815* (Tuscaloosa: University of Alabama Press, 2000), 30–34; and Jason Edward Black, "Memories of the Alabama Creek War, 1813–1814: U.S. Government and Native Identities at the Horseshoe Bend National Military Park," *American Indian Quarterly* 33, no. 2 (spring 2009): 200–229.

163. In the manuscript this is the second entry for August 17th, probably a diarist's error.

164. Chief Pathkiller (c. 1742–1827); principal chief from 1810 to 1827; perhaps the most influential leader of the Cherokees next to John Ross before forced removal in 1838–39. Various Cherokee spellings of the name are Naohetahee and Nunnahidilhi, which may mean "he kills in the path." He signed treaties of 1804 and 1805 and succeeded Black Fox in 1810; he was commissioned a colonel in the Creek War; however, this was only an honorific award. Besides leading the nation through the Creek War, he led the nation through the Creek Path conspiracy and the 1827 White Path Rebellion. In times of extreme uncertainty and suspense, Pathkiller was unyielding in the struggle for the retention of the ancestral domain by promoting the political centralization of Cherokee government. Upon his death in 1827, Charles Hicks ascended to principal chief, an office he held for one week before his death. McLoughlin, *Cherokee Renascence in the New Republic*, 125–58, 269, 389; and Moulton, *Papers of John Ross*, 2:729.

165. English in the German manuscript.

166. The reason the Cherokees decided to go against Creeks in war was to save Pathkiller from the unfriendly Creek faction, who was threatening him.

167. Although the Moravians disapproved Hicks's actions, they cautiously gave their consent for him to go to war against the Creeks. To show their further disdain for combat, the missionaries bemoaned the fact that women and children will be left behind. "For those who are willing to go and fight but did not have guns, Colonel Meigs advised them to ask a friend for one. The Flea asked us to lend him ours." Correspondence, John Gambold to Lewis David von Schweinitz, October 3, 1813, MAS.

168. Charles Hicks wrote from Turkeytown that General Andrew Jackson's detachment had attacked the Creeks some twenty-five miles from Springplace and killed 180 Creeks. However, the Cherokee detachment arrived too late to see action. Eighty Creeks were taken prisoner, and some of those escaped but were caught by Cherokee soldiers. Correspondence, John Gambold to Jacob Van Vleck, November 19, 1813, MAS.

169. One son was The Fish; the other son is unknown.

170. Susanna Wicked Ridge.

171. However, the soldiers demanded fodder for their horses. John Gambold to Jacob Van Vleck, November 19, 1813, MAS.

172. George Harlan, of present-day Cartersville, Georgia; son of Ellis and Catherine Harlan, daughter of Nancy Ward.

173. Wife of George Fields; siblings are James, Ann, and John Brown, children of Robert Brown of Chickamauga; mother of Springplace Mission pupils Archibald and Susan Fields.

174. The Bark, of Hightower (Etowah); great uncle or grandfather of Moravian student George Vann, son of John Vann and Polly Terrapin, daughter of Chief Terrapin; half-brother of Charles and John Beamer, a member of the National Council. For more information, see McClinton, *Moravian Springplace Mission to the Cherokees*, 2:456.

175. John Beamer of Hightower (Etowah); half-brother of The Bark and brother of Charles Beamer.

176. Moses McDonald.

177. Dick Justice, son of Dry Head and Jenny of Saliquoi and grandson of Charles and Tsowaeyakee of Saliquoi; well-known conjuror and chief; given the name Dik,keh (Dikkeh), which meant "The Just" but Anglo-Americans called him Justice. He was a delegate for the Treaty of 1816 at Turkeytown that established the Cherokee-Creek boundary as a result of the Creek War; owned a ferry at the juncture of the Federal Road and Tennessee River, near present-day Chattanooga. In 1819 Justice joined Arkansas Cherokees to escape Christianity and white intruders. Several of his family members stayed behind, and his son George Justice, living near Ross's Landing, suffered heavy losses due to forced removal in 1838–39. See Penelope Allen, "Manuscript of the History of the Cherokee Indians," 521–27; McLoughlin, *Cherokee Renascence in the New Republic*, 60, 210; and Charles Royce, "Cherokee Nations of Indians: A Narrative of Their Official Relations with the Colonial and Federal Governments," *Fifth Annual Report of the Bureau of Ethnology for the Secretary of the Smithsonian Institution* (Washington DC: U.S. Government Printing Office, 1887), 81–83.

2. Continuity of Traditional Cherokee Cultural Traits

1. See Amy Rogaris's introduction and chapter 3, "Models of Piety," in *Moral Geographer: Maps, Missionaries, and the American Frontier* (New York: Columbia University Press, 2003), for similar impressions of twenty-nine Connecticut Missionary Society accounts sent to Western Reserve between 1798 and 1818.

2. Stuart Banner, *How the Indians Lost their Lands: Law and Order on the Frontier* (Cambridge MA: Harvard University Press, 2005), 144.

3. François André Michaux, *Travels to the West of the Allegheny Mountains, in the States of Ohio, Kentucky, and Tennessea, and back to Charleston, by the Upper Carolinas*, 2nd ed. (London: D. N. Shury, 1805), 235.

4. Banner, *How the Indians Lost their Lands*, 190. In *Strother v. Cathey* (1807), North Carolina Supreme Court judge David Stone argued that the federal government could not have purchased fee simple title from the Cherokees because no government, European, U.S., or North Carolina, considered Indian title other than mere "possessory right."

5. Raymond D. Fogelson, "Perspectives on Native American Identity," in *Studying Native America: Problems and Prospects*, ed. Russell Thornton (Madison: University of Wisconsin Press, 1997), 48.

6. Shoemaker, *A Strange Likeness: Becoming Red and White in Eighteenth-Century North America* (New York: Oxford University Press, 2004), 21. Shoemaker contends that since Europeans divided their sense of space, they developed precise geometric and scientific systems to survey land; thus surveying land led to individual ownership.

7. Shoemaker, *Strange Likeness*, 15. Shoemaker points out that Cronon, in *Changes in the Land*, argues that Europeans viewed land in capitalistic terms and therefore were at total odds with the Indian subsistence level of land use. Cronin contends that Indians thought of their land use as a "customary" right to use land resources.

8. The early nineteenth-century term *yunek* may correspond to the Cherokee *Yo,ne,gi* (white person).

9. Correspondence, Abraham Steiner to Christian Lewis Benzien, August 18, 1801, Box M-411, MAS.

10. The diarist translates the Cherokee notion of God using the German *Gott*, not Great Spirit. Great Spirit is mentioned one time in the Springplace Diary, on September 17, 1820.

11. Early in 1811, the Cherokee National Council met and ordered all whites to leave the nation except a few blacksmiths and the Moravian missionaries. Others, including Vann's overseer, John Crawford, and a wagoner on Vann's estate, had to leave. They wanted Crawford removed because they said that he had stolen pigs and had built a house without the chiefs' permission. So they took all of his

possessions and made it impossible for him to return to his home. Correspondence, Gottlieb Byhan to Christian Lewis Benzien, March 6, 1811, MAS.

12. Wife of Vann's former overseer.

13. Dick Dyeentohee, former Springplace Mission student and son of Dick and Goadi of Chickamauga, grandson of The Flea.

14. Chief Koychezetel, Cherokee leader known also as Warrior's Nephew, was the husband of The Trunk's sister; also known for his stands on Cherokee nationalism.

15. Chief Warrior's Nephew's revelation to the missionaries was a harbinger of coming events. In September of 1811 a group of Shawnees, Choctaws, Cherokees, and a few unidentified Native persons met with Creek leaders at Tuckabatchee, the Upper Creek Town on the Tallapoosa River, and with Shawnee warrior Tecumseh. The Red Stick Creeks rallied behind the Shawnee leader's appeal for pan-Indian unity and resistance to Anglo-American encroachment. But Shawnee diplomacy failed to create pan-Indian nationalism among the Cherokees. Gregory E. Dowd, *A Spirited Resistance: The North American Struggle for Unity, 1745–1815* (Baltimore: John Hopkins University Press, 1992), 169–83; and Claudio Saunt, *A New Order of Things: Property, Power, and the Transformation of the Creek Indians, 1733–1816* (Cambridge: Cambridge University Press, 1999), 233–72. For further discourse on the Creek cultural resistance, see Kathryn E. Holland Braund, *Deerskins and Duffels: Creek Indian Trade with Anglo-America, 1685–1815* (Lincoln: University of Nebraska Press, 1993); and Green, *Politics of Indian Removal*. For an in-depth portrayal of Tecumseh's sojourn among the Creeks, see John Sugden, *Tecumseh: A Life* (New York: Henry Holt, 1997), 243–51. For a general study of Tecumseh's life, see R. David Edmunds, *Tecumseh and the Quest for Indian Leadership* (Boston: Little, Brown, 1984).

16. English in the German manuscript. For example, Old Chota and Tugalo.

17. For Cherokee attitudes toward violent punishment, see Gregory D. Dowd, "Gift Giving and the Cherokee-British Alliance," in *Contact Points: American Frontiers from the Mohawk Valley to the Mississippi, 1750–1830*, ed. Andrew R. L. Cayton and Fredrika J. Teute (Chapel Hill: University of North Carolina Press, 1998), 127–31. For British attitudes toward corporal punishment, see Lawrence Stone, *The Crisis of the Aristocracy, 1558–1641* (Oxford: Clarendon Pres, 1965), 35, 680–81.

18. James Blair.

19. English in the German manuscript.

20. Most Cherokees and chiefs opposed the enrollment for removal of Cherokee citizens to Arkansas and the taking out of reserves, provisions of the Treaty of

1818. Tennessee governor Joseph McMinn asked Colonel Meigs to call a Council meeting to upbraid chiefs for their opposition. Cherokee leaders refused to attend, and McMinn accused them of threatening lives of ones who would possibly convene. To protest these and other improper actions, the Cherokees called a Council at Oostanaula from June 20 to July 3, in the wake of a possible threat by McMinn to withhold annuity payments. These heightened concerns dominated Cherokee leadership from the middle of April to the time of the Council meeting. See McLoughlin, *Cherokee Renascence in the New Republic*, 234–40.

21. Tiya Miles and Theda Perdue and Michael D. Green have quoted from this 1818 presentation which Margaret Scott Vann Crutchfield made before the Cherokee Council. See Miles, "'Circular Reasoning': Recentering Cherokee Women in the Antiremoval Campaigns," *American Quarterly* 61, no. 2 (June 2009): 231; and Perdue and Green, *The Cherokee Removal: A Brief History with Documents*, 2nd ed. (Boston: Bedford/St. Martin's, 2005), 132–33.

22. This entry is from a letter from John Gambold to Jacob Van Vleck, March 18, 1819, Moravian Archives, Salem.

23. According to anthropologist Raymond D. Fogelson, the new and old fires refer to the end of a new era and the beginning of another. Private conversation with editor, April 2002.

24. Edwards, *Memoir of the Rev. Elias Cornelius*, 87. See also Mrs. Anna Gambold, "Plants of the Cherokee Country: 'A list of plants found in the neighborhood of Connasarga River, (Cherokee Country), where Springplace is situated," *American Journal of Science* 1:245–51; and John Witthoft, *Journal of the Washington Academy of Sciences*, vol. 37, no. 3 (March 15, 1947): 73–75.

25. Collin G. Calloway, *New Worlds for All: Indians, Europeans, and the Remaking of Early America* (Baltimore: Johns Hopkins University Press, 1997), 20.

26. Nancy Shoemaker, *A Strange Likeness*, 107.

27. R. Douglas Hurt, *Indian Agriculture in American: Prehistory to the Present* (Lawrence: University Press of Kansas, 1987), 87.

28. Vann overseer William Crawford; took Josiah Vann's place.

29. Jim Foster (c. 1780–c. 1846), son of Nancy (Ga,ho,ga) Lightfoot and James Foster.

30. The Ridge and his brother David Watie.

31. Robin (c. 1801), son of James Vann or Water Hunter and Dawnee (below Oostanaula); entered the mission school November 20, 1815; dismissed for bad behavior in 1818.

32. Consult Theda Perdue's "Constructing Gender," chapter 1 of *Cherokee*

Women: Gender and Culture Change, 1700–1835 (Lincoln: University of Nebraska Press, 1998).

33. English [unedited] in the German manuscript.

34. William Shorey Hicks.

35. Postmenopausal women, believed to have special power, often undertook the art of healing and conjuring. Cherokees believed that bodily fluids such as breath, saliva, and blood were anomalous and thus had mystical properties. The blowing or spraying of the medicine was performed externally even if the origin of the disease was internal. James Mooney and Fran Olbrechts, "The Swimmer Manuscript: Cherokee Sacred Formulas and Medicinal Properties," *Bureau of American Ethnology Bulletin 99*, (Washington DC: U.S. Government Printing Office, 1932), 34, 58–60, 84. Hereafter cited as "The Swimmer Manuscript."

36. See "The Use of Alcohol" in chapter 1.

37. Sons of Onai and Gunrod.

38. Or Dorcas. Daughter of The Rattling Gourd and Polly of Big Spring, near Springplace Mission.

39. "The Rattling Gourd . . . had a turkey feather that he used to sweep the schoolroom. During the school sessions, he sat next to Anna Rosina and between classes he talked in Indian language. He was completely unconcerned that we do not understand him. But when he wants to know something, he makes himself intelligible to us. He does not speak any English." John Gambold to Jacob Van Vleck, August 26, 1814, MAS

40. Polly Toney Rattling Gourd.

41. Toney.

42. After Darkey left Springplace, John Gambold wrote that he heard that Darkey "lived with an old relative and sold corn and brandy for her father." Correspondence, John Gambold to Jacob Van Vleck, January 4, 1816, MAS.

43. Waterhunter was a husband of Dawnee, mother of Moravian student Robin, who entered Springplace in 1815. Robin's father was probably James Vann.

44. Sumach was a town some ten miles north of Diamond Hill.

45. Dawnee.

46. The Little Boys' Covenant Day.

47. Charles Hudson, *The Southeastern Indians* (Knoxville: University of Tennessee Press, 1976; reprint, 1992), 199.

48. John "Hellfire Jack" Rogers.

49. Elizabeth Emory and her daughter, Jennie Due, Rogers's stepdaughter.

50. Moses and Robert Parris.

51. George Parris.

52. Daughter of George.

53. George Vann.

54. Peggy and Joseph Crutchfield.

55. Will was the Crutchfields' slave.

56. The Gambolds related that in the case of illness and preparation for ball play, Cherokees hired conjurors, but usually not to cast spells. The Gambolds learned more about spells from Peggy Wolf, who told how "her brother and sister had to sit on the floor until the conjuror bathed them in water to rid them of a spell."

57. The Cherokee ceremony "going to water." Lee Irwin, "Cherokee Healing: Myth, Dreams, and Medicine," *American Indian Quarterly* 16 (Spring 1992): 237–57; and James Mooney, "The Cherokee River Cult," *Journal of American Folklore* 13 (January–March 1900): 1–10.

58. Polly Blackwood entered Brainerd mission school June 8, 1818; the missionaries listed her as respectable and knowledgeable about reading and writing. Phillips and Phillips, *Brainerd Journal*, 406, 450.

59. Sally McDonald was the widow of George McDonald, son of John and Anne Shorey McDonald.

60. Caty, slave belonging to Margaret (Peggy) Scott Vann.

61. Josiah Vann.

62. Peter, Bob, and Isaac.

63. Son of missionaries Gottlieb and Dorothea Byhan.

64. "[A]nd as the person who brings the corpse to the place of burial, immediately leave it, he is at liberty to dispose of all as he pleases, but must take care never to be found out, as nothing belonging to the dead is to be kept, but every thing at his decease destroyed, except these articles, which destined to accompany him to the other world." *The Memoirs of Lt. Henry Timberlake: The Story of a Soldier, Adventurer, and Emissary to the Cherokees, 1756–1765*, ed. Duane H. King (Cherokee NC: Museum of the Cherokee Indian Press, 2007), 35.

65. Calhgio of Spring Place.

66. Charles Hicks was the nephew of The Gunrod, whose sister was probably Charles Hicks's mother, signifying the efficacy of matrilineal descent.

67. Or Koychezetel.

68. Springplace neighbor The Trunk's sister.

69. Hudson, *Southeastern Indians*, 338.

70. Johnny Gutseyedi of Hightower.

71. According to former assistant deputy chief and the late Hastings Shade of the Cherokee Nation, hunters of ancient times fasted four days before they went on hunting forays. Hunting deer required a chant, and even some venison was left at the site of the kill so that deer never became scarce. Hastings Shade, "Myths and Legends, and Old Sayings" (privately published by Hastings Shade, 1994), 55–56.

72. *Reinlichen*; loving cleanliness.

73. The Cherokees divided themselves into seven matrilineal clans, Wolf, Bird, Deer, Paint, Long Hair, Blind Savannah, and Holly, and the members of a particular clan claimed descent from a single unknown ancestor. Since clan membership ran into the thousands, the Cherokees claimed kin to many people. Unlike the matrilineage, the clan lacked an economic basis, but the clan provided social bonds so strong that aboriginal Cherokees needed no further political structure. John Phillip Reid, *A Law of Blood: The Primitive Law of the Cherokee Nation* (New York: New York University Press, 1970), 189, 191. Refer also to Strickland's *Fire and the Spirits*.

74. Reid, *Law of Blood*, 37.

75. *Laws of the Cherokee Nation Adopted by the Council at Various Periods* (Tahlequah, Cherokee Nation: Cherokee Advocate Office, 1853; reprint, Wilmington DE: Scholarly Resources, 1973), 4.

76. The extent to which the Nation replaced the clan system is questionable. V. Richard Persico Jr., "Early Nineteenth-Century Cherokee Political Organization," *The Cherokee Indian Nation: A Troubled History*, ed. Duane H. King (Knoxville: University of Tennessee Press, 1979), 105.

77. Timothy Alan Garrison, *The Legal Ideology of Removal: The Southern Judiciary and the Sovereignty of Native American Nations* (Athens: University of Georgia Press, 2002), 38–39.

78. Garrison, *Legal Ideology of Removal*, 51. Their presence may have related to an earlier incident reported by Chiquaki, Johnny Gutseysdi's grandfather, in which two Indians who had stolen horses had both eyes put out with a penknife and each received one hundred lashes.

79. John Falling.

80. Rumor had it that Vann would be killed on his return trip from Washington. Correspondence, John Gambold to Carl Gotthold Reichel, January 19, 1806, MAS.

81. John Tynor was a wagoner and one-time Vann overseer.

82. In March of 1806 at a Council meeting at Oostanaula, Falling, who was drinking, said that Vann's slaves, who had stolen his money, had deposited eight hundred dollars with him (Falling). The delegates told him to return the money to Vann. Then Falling denied collusion. Correspondence, John and Anna Rosina Gambold to Christian Lewis Benzien, April 20, 1806, MAS.

83. Doublehead.

84. Cherokee law ("Cry Blood") dictated that the clan of the one killed avenge for wrongs. In 1810, the Cherokee Council revised clan retaliation. *Laws of the Cherokee Nation*, 4.

85. Nancy Vann Falling. Because of possible clan reprisal, Nancy feared that Falling's relatives would kill her. John and Anna Rosina Gambold to Christian Lewis Benzien, May 25, 1806, MAS; and *Laws of the Cherokee Nation*, 4.

86. Anna Rosina Gambold described his daughter as a "half-brown little girl" who understood both English and Cherokee and claimed she would live with them.

87. Elizabeth Emory.

88. Archibald Fields's father, George Fields of Big Spring near the mission, was a relative of the deceased John Falling. Archibald's mother was Jenny Vann Fields. Correspondence, Anna Rosina Gambold to Mrs. Christian Lewis Benzien, July 22, 1806, MAS.

89. Distant Dew, also known as Morning Dew, was the son of Susanna and Otterlifter of Sumach.

90. Squatisele was the son of Tuhsiwalliti of Conasauga; mother unknown.

91. *aus demselben Stammen.*

92. See section on "Ball Play" for an explanation of the Cherokee ceremony.

93. Jonathan Blacke, one of Gideon Blackburn's schoolteachers.

94. "The Ridge shot him but did not kill him and the next day, Alexander Saunders planted a tomahawk in his skull—the rest fell upon him and chopped his head to pieces." John Howard Payne Papers, 2:28–30, Ayer Collection, Newberry Library, Chicago.

95. Doublehead had sided with Indian agent Meigs when he sold Cherokee lands to whites and encouraged fellow Cherokees to do the same. The Ridge and Charles Hicks opposed these actions, and Meigs from then on called the anti-Doublehead faction "patriots" and subsequently fired Hicks as the official interpreter for the Cherokee Indian Agency. Some reported that Doublehead had severely beaten his wife, a sister of one of Vann's wives. McLoughlin, *Cherokee Renascence*, 101–5, 120–21; and Wilkins, *Cherokee Tragedy*, 36.

96. His business partner was John Chisholm. When asked why Cherokees had not reported to Meigs about Doublehead's unlawful dealings with whites, it was said that Colonel Meigs was "as bad as them, meaning Doublehead and Chisholm." McLoughlin, *Cherokee Renascence*, 121.

97. Vann's reputation for exacting cruel and excessive punishments as a participant in the Cherokee light horse brigade (or Cherokee constabulary) led to personal retributions against him. McLoughlin, *Cherokee Renascence*, 151.

98. Alexander Saunders probably shot Vann. Once they had been best of friends, but Vann made him an enemy because of malicious insults. Correspondence, John Gambold to Christian Lewis Benzien, February 23, 1809, MAS.

99. Joseph Vann.

100. Vann owned a store, tavern, and another plantation at the juncture of the Federal Road and Chattahoochee River, where the now damned Chattahoochee River has created Lake Lanier.

101. Tom Buffington's tavern on the Federal Road.

102. Johnston McDonald.

103. The Gambolds regretted they did not know this behavior was taking place. Every morning Anna Rosina Gambold asked the children how they slept and if anyone had quarreled. John Ridge had told his visiting father that Johnny had pricked and scratched Buck with a stickpin. "Johnny refused to recant; he just scratched behind his ears." Correspondence, John Gambold to Christian Lewis Benzien, May 20, 1811, MAS.

104. He lived in Hightower.

105. Albert J. Raboteau, *Slave Religion: The Invisible Institution in the Antebellum South* (New York: Oxford University Press, 1978; reprint, 1980), 276.

106. Fred Gearing, *Priests and Warriors: Social Structures for Cherokee Politics in the 18th Century*, Memoir 93, American Anthropological Association, vol. 64, no. 5, pt. 2 (1962), 31; and Alan Kilpatrick, *The Night Has a Naked Soul: Witchcraft and Sorcery among the Western Cherokee* (Syracuse NY: Syracuse University Press, 1997), 126.

107. Kilpatrick, *Night Has a Naked Soul*, 126.

108. Gearing, "Priests and Warriors," 31.

109. John Gambold related that in the case of illness and preparation for ball play, Cherokees hired conjurors, but usually not to cast spells. The Gambolds learned more about spells from Peggy Wolf, who told how "her brother and sister had to sit on the floor until the conjuror bathed them in water to rid them of a spell." One shamanistic category concerned those individuals who could use their skills and knowledge to harm other people. The most notorious causes of disease were those begun by these infamous practitioners, who were "of a different mind"; they could cause illness or even death through uncommon formulaic utterances. Sometimes shamans hid along a trail and waited for the victim to spit. After they gathered the saliva, conjurors employed the correct formula to cause a fatal sickness. Sometimes the practitioner produced powerful spells to steal a person's soul or to "ravish" it by inducing suffering for six or seven months before dying. Lee Irwin, "Cherokee Healing: Myth, Dreams, and Medicine," 245.

110. Perhaps, in an attempt to protect her son from what anthropologist Lucy Mair refers to an "unneighborly person," she hired a conjuror to cast a spell on the Moravians, whom she believed had harmed him. Mair describes "unneighborly person" as "the one whom one would not wish to resemble and

also the one whom one should avoid offending." Lucy Mair, *Witchcraft* (New York: McGraw-Hill, 1969), 202.

111. Cherokee scholar Fred Gearing pointed out that "direct, open conflict" caused injury to one's reputation, so to avoid harm, Cherokees used indirect methods to resolve disputes and restore the "harmony ethic." Conjurors played this role skillfully. Gearing, "Priests and Warriors," 31.

112. Margaret Ann Scott Vann Crutchfield.

113. Cherokees refrained from using corporal punishment. For more information concerning attitudes about corporal punishment, see Hudson, *Southeastern Indians*, 323–24; and Theda Perdue, *The Cherokee* (New York: Chelsea House, 1989), 16–17.

114. Dawzizi or David Steiner (David Taucheechy, Tarcheechee, Taurcheechey, Datsisi, or Dazizi) (c. 1798); son of The Tyger and Oodeisaski (Smith) of Big Spring; age twelve; entered the mission school September 20, 1810; departed August 18, 1817. In 1817 Dawzizi left Springplace Mission at the request of The Tyger; later when he converted to Christianity, and he received the name David Steiner Taucheechy. He went to Cornwall in 1818 and stayed until 1822. Then he returned to the Springplace Mission and requested full membership into the Moravian Church, only to be repeatedly rejected. He then applied at Brainerd, became a Presbyterian, and served as an interpreter with Brainerd. Schwarze, *History of the Moravian Missions*, 171.

115. According to anthropologist Raymond D. Fogelson, the fish mentioned is probably a garfish, which are abundant in the riverine Southeast (personal communication with editor, October 28, 2000).

116. Sam D. Gill, *Native American Religions: An Introduction* (BelmontCA: Wadsworth, 1982), 130–33; and Garrison, *Legal Ideology of Removal*, 7.

117. *Hausvater*. Cherokee headman; the literal translation of the term for principal man of the house.

118. In 1818 second principal chief Charles Hicks wrote: "Before eating the green corn when in the milk, the people collect in the different towns and villages at night, and . . . the conjuror takes some of the grains of seven ears of corn and feeds the fire with them, i.e., burns them. After this each family is allowed to cook and eat their roasting-ears, but not before they drink a tea of wild horehound. John R. Swanton, *The Indians of the Southeastern United States*, Bureau of American Ethnology, Bulletin 137 (Washington DC: U.S. Government Printing Office, 1946), 771. For a similar translation, see Clemens de Baillou, "A Contribution to the Mythology and Conceptual World of the Cherokee Indians," *Ethnohistory* 8 (1981): 95–96. For more information on the Green Corn Dance, see John Witthoft, *Green Corn Ceremonialism in the Eastern United States*, Occasional

Contribution from the Museum of Anthropology of the University of Michigan, no. 13 (Ann Arbor: University of Michigan Press, 1949), 4–5.

119. James Mooney, "The Cherokee Ball Play," *Journal of Cherokee Studies* 7, no. 1 (Spring 1982): 11–13, 18–21. See also James Adair, *Adair's History of the American Indians*, ed. Samuel Cole Williams (1930; reprint, New York: Promontory Press, 1974), 428–31; and Raymond Fogelson, "The Cherokee Ballgame Cycle: An Ethnographer's View," *Journal of the Society for Musicology* 15 (September 1971): 327–38.

120. J. P. Evans, "Sketches of Cherokee Characteristics," *Journal of Cherokee Studies* 4 (Winter 1979): 15–16.

121. Charles and Tsowaeyakee of Saliquoi (Salacoa) at the confluence of the Salacoa Creek and the Oostanaula River.

122. Johnston McDonald.

123. The Tyger (Tiger), took part in the 1827 White Path's Rebellion, an antimission and antiwestern movement orchestrated to restore Cherokee traditions. However, to show Cherokee solidarity, he signed a resolution to support the new Cherokee Constitution in 1827; son of an Onondaga; husband of Oodeisaski Smith, with whom he had numerous children: Dawzizi (David Steiner), Redbird, Messenger, who married Celia Love, Pelican, Mark, who married Mary Thompson and another woman by the name Stidham (née Trott), Ticanohila (Ti,ca,no,hila), who married Edmund (Rock) Crutchfield, Dirttower, Kahita (Ka,hi,ta), Walia (Wa,li,a), and Lucretia, who married Tony Rattling Gourd, son of The Rattling Gourd and Polly Toney. McLoughlin, *Cherokee Renascence*, 394–95; and Starr, *History of the Cherokee Indians*, 452.

124. Harlan's mill was approximately twenty miles from Springplace. Correspondence, John Gambold to Lewis David von Schweinitz, January 12, 1813, MAS.

125. The fields where ball play took place bordered the spring-fed branch of the Conasauga River adjacent to Springplace.

126. Oodeisaski (Oo,du,ski) Smith.

127. Pelican.

128. John Gambold's brother, Joseph Gambold, a widower, arrived at Springplace in 1808 and stayed for twenty years.

129. According to anthropologist Fogelson, milk caused an allergic reaction among Cherokees, but The Tyger's heritage was Onondaga.

130. Peggy Vann Crutchfield and Joseph Crutchfield lived at Mountjoy, about three miles from Springplace.

131. Possibly the root from a wild crabapple tree that brought luck during ball play. Mooney, "The Cherokee Ball Play," 20.

132. The entries of September 22 and 23, 1817, demonstrate threatened retaliation

from property settlements, a topic that could be included under "Cherokee Law and Punishment." Sister Crutchfield's father, Walter Scott, had left his property, mainly slaves, to his widow and stipulated that she should leave this property to their children. When Mrs. Scott married Robert Brown, he took the property after she died and distributed the wealth among his children by a previous marriage. One of the Brown relatives, John Brown, told Crutchfield that if he demanded any money from the sale of the property, he would beat him up. Correspondence, John Gambold to Simon Peter, October 17, 1817, MAS. The National Committee with John Ross as president made the following decision: "The National Committee have taken into consideration the controversy between the heirs of Walter Scott, deceased, and their half sisters, the Browns, relating to the right of property defended from the said deceased Walter Scott, and are of opinion that Mrs. Sarah Brown as widow to Walter Scott deceased, ought to be entitled to her dower. Therefore they have decided that the property given by Mrs. Sarah Brown deceased to her daughters, viz.: to Katy Doublehead three hundred dollars and fifty dollars cash; to Charlotte Brown, one Negro Girl Betty & to Ibby Brown, one negro woman named Nan and her child, shall be considered as lawful heirs to the above named property given to them by their mother Mrs. Sarah Brown, deceased." National Committee, John Ross, President, and Alex McCoy, Clerk, November 26, 1818, John Howard Payne Papers, 7:40, Ayer Collection, Newberry Library, Chicago.

133. John Brown went home from ball play without going by Brother Crutchfield's house. Correspondence, John Gambold to Simon Peter, October 17, 1817, MAS.

134. The Messenger (about thirteen years old).

135. Pelican (about nine years old).

136. John Gambold and Johann Renatus Schmidt.

137. Johann Renatus Schmidt.

138. The Elk is mentioned also in McLoughlin, *Cherokee Renascence in the New Republic*, 176–77; McLoughlin, "The Cherokees Use of Christianity," in *The Cherokees and Christianity, 1794–1870: Essays on Acculturation and Cultural Persistence*, Walter Conser, ed. (Athens: University of Georgia Press, 1994), 168–69; and Claudio Saunt, "Telling Stories: The Political Uses of Myth and History in the Cherokee and Creek Nations," *Journal of American History* vol. 93, no. 3(2006): 673–98.

139. Linda Tuhiwai Smith, *Decolonizing Methodologies: Research and Indigenous Peoples* (London: University of Otago Press, 2001), 72–74.

140. Uniluchfty was from Fortville, some eighteen miles directly west of Springplace; the Cherokees built a fort there for security purposes and named the Indian settlement Fortville.

141. It was not until the early 1820s that the Cherokees became literate through Sequoyah's invention of the syllabary and could correspond with each other. The Cherokees relied on missionaries to help them write official letters in English.

142. Colonel Return Jonathan Meigs of the Hiwassee Agency.

143. You here is personal the *Du*.

144. Tuckabatchie (which has many variant spellings in the Springplace Diary) was a ravaged Creek town where in September of 1815, U.S. commissioners Colonels Benjamin Hawkins and William Barnett (General John Sevier was too sick to attend) called a Council meeting with the Creeks. Because the ceded Creek land included Cherokee territory, the Cherokees were also present. Wilkins, *Cherokee Tragedy*, 86–87; and October 31, 1815, and November 4, 1815, Letters Received, Records of the Cherokee Indian Agency in Tennessee, 1801–35, Record Group 75, M208, roll 6, National Archives.

145. The Elk's story held further relevance for the Cherokees because he explained the significance of Cherokees' attachment to the land and the source of food. Later, the Cherokee informant Swimmer explained to ethnologist James Mooney that the first man and woman, Kanati and Selu, held the secrets to the origin of the hunt for game and the mystery surrounding the growing of corn. In 1888 Mooney interviewed Swimmer, a noted Cherokee shaman, antiquarian, and storyteller of Cherokee, North Carolina, and a member of the Eastern Band. Swimmer, who did not speak English, knew Sequoyah's syllabary, and provided Mooney with the most extensive record of sacred formulas and Cherokee myths recorded in syllabary up to that time. Donned always in his traditional turban and moccasins, his legacy was enromous. He died in 1889 at the age of sixty-five. Mooney, *Myths of the Cherokee and Sacred Formulas of the Cherokees*, Nineteenth and Seventh Annual Reports of the Bureau of American Ethnology (1900, 1891; Nashville: Charles and Randy Elder Booksellers, 1982), 137–38.

146. The story implied that the "bad intention" was her boys' threat on her life because they thought she was a sorceress.

147. Another translation for trade and commerce: thrive and strive. The Elk story predated the "Swimmer Manuscript" and Sickatowah. In these stories, no mention is made of the "book of trade and traffic or a book on thrive and strive." John Howard Payne Papers, 1:26–31, Ayer Collection, Newberry Library, Chicago. See also Mooney, "Myths of the Cherokees," Bureau of American Ethnology, *Nineteenth Annual Report, 1897–98*, 243–49.

148. James P. Ronda, "We Are Well as We Are: An Indian Critique of Seventeenth-Century Christian Missions," *William and Mary Quarterly*, 3rd ser., 34 (January 1977): 76–78. For recently published articles regarding other colonial encounters with Indians, see David J. Silverman, "Indians, Missionaries, and

Religious Translation: Creating Wampanoag Christianity in Seventeenth-Century Martha's Vineyard," *William and Mary Quarterly*, 3rd ser., 62 (April 2005): 141–74; and Silverman, "The Curse of God: An Idea and Its Origins among the Indians of New York's Revolutionary Frontier," *William and Mary Quarterly*, 3rd ser., 66 (July 2009): 495–534.

149. James Axtell, *The Invasion Within: The Contest of Cultures in Colonial North America* (New York: Oxford University Press, 1985), 19.

150. Or Ode.

151. Usually translated as "hello," "good," or "satisfied."

Epilogue

1. John Ridge to President James Monroe, March 8, 1821, Box 761, Ayer Collection, Newberry Library.

2. Garrison, *Legal Ideology of Removal*, 7.

3. Elias Cornelius, corresponding secretary of the Prudential Committee of the American Board of Commissioners for Foreign Missions.

4. Cyrus Kingsbury, American Board of Commissioners for Foreign Missions, and missionary to the Choctaws.

5. Correspondence, John Gambold to Jacob Van Vleck, February 18, 1818, MAS.

6. Correspondence, Johann Renatus Schmidt to Andrew Benade, November 11, 1824, MAS.

In the Indians of the Southeast series

The Payne-Butrick Papers,
Volumes 1, 2, 3
Edited and annotated by
William L. Anderson, Jane L. Brown,
and Anne F. Rogers

The Payne-Butrick Papers,
Volumes 4, 5, 6
Edited and annotated by
William L. Anderson, Jane L. Brown,
and Anne F. Rogers

Deerskins and Duffels
The Creek Indian Trade
with Anglo-America, 1685–1815
By Kathryn E. Holland Braund

Searching for the Bright Path
The Mississippi Choctaws from
Prehistory to Removal
By James Taylor Carson

Demanding the Cherokee Nation
Indian Autonomy and American
Culture, 1830–1900
By Andrew Denson

The Second Creek War
Interethnic Conflict and Collusion
on a Collapsing Frontier
By John T. Ellisor

Cherokee Americans
The Eastern Band of Cherokees
in the Twentieth Century
By John R. Finger

Creeks and Southerners
Biculturalism on the
Early American Frontier
By Andrew K. Frank

Choctaw Genesis, 1500–1700
By Patricia Galloway

The Southeastern Ceremonial Complex
Artifacts and Analysis
The Cottonlandia Conference
Edited by Patricia Galloway
Exhibition Catalog by
David H. Dye and Camille Wharey

The Invention of the
Creek Nation, 1670–1763
By Steven C. Hahn

Bad Fruits of the Civilized Tree
Alcohol and the Sovereignty of
the Cherokee Nation
By Izumi Ishii

Epidemics and Enslavement
Biological Catastrophe in the
Native Southeast, 1492–1715
By Paul Kelton

An Assumption of Sovereignty
Social and Political Transformation
among the Florida Seminoles, 1953–1979
By Harry A. Kersey Jr.

The Caddo Chiefdoms
Caddo Economics and Politics, 700–1835
By David La Vere

The Moravian Springplace Mission
to the Cherokees, Volume 1: 1805–1813
The Moravian Springplace Mission
to the Cherokees, Volume 2: 1814–1821
Edited and introduced
by Rowena McClinton

The Moravian Springplace Mission to the Cherokees, Abridged Edition
Edited and with an introduction by Rowena McClinton

Keeping the Circle
American Indian Identity in Eastern North Carolina, 1885–2004
By Christopher Arris Oakley

Choctaws in a Revolutionary Age, 1750–1830
By Greg O'Brien

Cherokee Women
Gender and Culture Change, 1700–1835
By Theda Perdue

The Brainerd Journal
A Mission to the Cherokees, 1817–1823
Edited and introduced by Joyce B. Phillips and Paul Gary Phillips

Seminole Voices
Reflections on Their Changing Society, 1970–2000
By Julian M. Pleasants and Harry A. Kersey Jr.

The Yamasee War
A Study of Culture, Economy, and Conflict in the Colonial South
By William L. Ramsey

The Cherokees
A Population History
By Russell Thornton

Buffalo Tiger
A Life in the Everglades
By Buffalo Tiger and Harry A. Kersey Jr.

American Indians in the Lower Mississippi Valley
Social and Economic Histories
By Daniel H. Usner Jr.

William Bartram on the Southeastern Indians
Edited and annotated by Gregory A. Waselkov and Kathryn E. Holland Braund

Powhatan's Mantle
Indians in the Colonial Southeast
Edited by Peter H. Wood, Gregory A. Waselkov, and M. Thomas Hatley

Creeks and Seminoles
The Destruction and Regeneration of the Muscogulge People
By J. Leitch Wright Jr.

Breinigsville, PA USA
27 September 2010

246180BV00002B/2/P